Battleground Europe
FLESQUIÈRES

Battleground Europe

FLESQUIÈRES

Jack Horsfall & Nigel Cave
with the assistance of Philippe Gorczynski

Series editor
Nigel Cave

LEO COOPER

First published in 2003 by
LEO COOPER
an imprint of
Pen Sword Books Limited
47 Church Street, Barnsley, South Yorkshire S70 2AS

Copyright © Jack Horsfall & Nigel Cave, 2003

ISBN 0 85052 897 6

A CIP catalogue of this book is available
from the British Library

Printed by CPI UK

*For up-to-date information on other titles produced under the Leo Cooper imprint,
please telephone or write to:*
Pen & Sword Books Ltd, FREEPOST, 47 Church Street
Barnsley, South Yorkshire S70 2AS
Telephone 01226 734222

CONTENTS

**British troops in
Flesquières after its
capture.**

Introduction by Series Editor

With this volume in the series the Battle of Cambrai has now been covered in the Battleground Europe series. Jack Horsfall has engaged in a real labour of love in preparing these books, and has had to display the patience of Job at the snail-like pace of myself as I fulfilled my end of the bargain. It would be remiss not to thank Philippe Gorczynski, of the Hotel Beatus in Cambrai and the Flesquières Tank Association, for his tremendous assistance in so many aspects of the preparation of this book; also his colleagues in the Association have been most helpful.

Cambrai was a battle with a lot of maybes and what ifs. It is chiefly remembered for tanks, though arguably the use of artillery was of more military impact. Certainly by the end of it and the Battle of Third Ypres the German High Command was left in a quandary as to the next military step they should take on the Western Front; and their next step, although meeting enormous success in terms of land gained, was the strategic error that enabled the war to be concluded in 1918 on the Allies' terms.

The countryside west of Cambrai is impressive and it is a more manageable battlefield than the Somme. Much of Britain's heaviest fighting took place in the fields around here in the years 1917 and 1918, and it is to be hoped that these books, along with those produced by Bill Mitchinson, Helen McPhail and Philip Guest; and the general book of the area by Peter Oldham, will have attracted more visitors here and will continue so to do.

The fighting at Flesquières was important not only for Cambrai itself, but in the winter of 1917 and the German spring offensive. In the case of the latter, the heroic defence by formations of the Fifth Army in this area proved to be a vital part in the foiling of the great German spring offensive of March 1918. As the war came to a conclusion – though this was not obvious at the time – the fighting in the region was an important part of the breaching of the formidable Hindenburg Line system, the collapse of which left the Germans bereft of a strong bastion upon which they could rest their battered troops. In this book Jack Horsfall has covered all of these areas. His tours cover the ground extensively; and he spends a great deal of the tours section on the often neglected cemeteries which hold the bodies of men of both sides who fought so bravely and heroically in appalling circumstance. This trilogy of books is a considerable tribute to these men.

Nigel Cave
Porta Latina, Rome

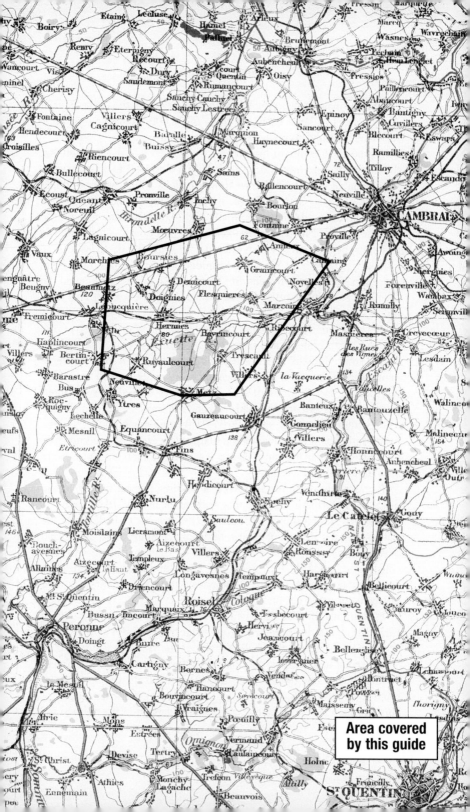

Area covered
by this guide

Introduction

The German army originally captured Cambrai in the heady days of August 1914, a large cathedral town of 28,000, connected by good roads and railways to many parts of France and back into Germany.

As the 1916 Battle of the Somme progressed into the late autumn, the Germans determined on establishing a line well to the rear; this would enable them to withdraw from positions which were no longer of their choosing and which required a disproportionate number of men to hold. In addition, the supply and logistics of the line on the Somme provided increasing problems. The solution was to move into positions, pre-prepared, which offered a resolution to these issues.

The Germans built the most formidable defence line Europe had ever seen. Between Arras and St Quentin the new line was called the Siegfried Stellung; the British called it the Hindenburg Line. This forty mile long section was formidable, but it was particularly so in front of Cambrai, where it passed about five miles to the west. From Arras the line ran south easterly and passed in front of Cambrai. That ancient walled town, famous for its three spires, had become the Germans' main base in the north. It was heavily industrialised, with numerous warehouses and factories. It was also connected to all parts of their front and into Germany by good road and rail links. Prior to the spring 1917 withdrawal, it lay some forty – fifty miles behind the Somme Front, safe from all but marauding planes. The area became known as the 'Flanders Sanatorium', where battered German divisions were brought to rest and re-equip.

Immediately south of the town is a hollow of about twenty square miles. The northern edge of this geographical bowl-like feature is enclosed by the Flesquières Ridge. Two miles north of that, across the flat land, is the straight Roman road from Cambrai to Bapaume; and beyond its northern side the 600 acres of Bourlon Wood, on a hill which rises to 150 feet from the Plain and can be seen from considerable distances away. It dominates the local countryside. The village of Bourlon lies on its northern side.

Flesquières sits in the centre of the five mile long ridge; Havrincourt lies two miles away, on the western end. Five miles south of Flesquières, across the shallow bowl, is the Bonavis Ridge. On its eastern edge is the valley through which flows the St Quentin Canal, 40 metres wide and three to four deep. This winds its way up from the south, curving through four villages in the bowl, until it comes due north through the western edge of Cambrai. Opposite, five miles to the west, is the Trescault Ridge (running north south) which frames the bowl. Immediately beyond it is Havrincourt Wood, which is very large and dense, consisting of about 2,000 acres. Nearby is the Canal du Nord, forty yards wide and ten yards deep – in one part thirty yards deep – running through the deep cutting at the western end of the Flesquières Ridge. In 1917 it was dry, forming a serious barrier to the Allies. South of this the canal runs through a two mile long tunnel between Ytres and Ruyaulcourt. Curving around the western edge of Havrincourt Wood it cuts through a deep gorge just west of Havrincourt and then proceeds to the north, almost parallel to the St Quentin Canal. They both flow into the Sensée River, six miles north of Cambrai. (The Canal du Nord, though largely dug before the war started in 1914, did not have barges travelling on it until 1963.)

In the centre, towards the bottom of the bowl, is Ribécourt. Roads emanated from the small village to all parts of the bowl; in fact it was in the middle of the 'Sanatorium'. The Germans used both canals, weaving the Hindenburg Line's massive trench and barbed wire systems into them. Here the Line was five miles deep, reaching eastwards to the St Quentin Canal. There were three rows of deep, inter-connected trenches purposely cut very wide to prevent tanks crossing them. Each trench was defended by heavy duty barbed wire in two hundred metre bands. There were concrete bunkers and large, strong dugouts, the whole so well constructed that no ordinary infantry attack had any hope of success.

The 'Flanders Sanatorium' was a safe place, so much so that the numbers of German infantry manning it were relatively few. They were second line units and there were never more than three divisions in the ten mile long length protecting Cambrai.

Meanwhile, on the British side of the wire, the tank had been deployed for the first time on 15 September, 1916 during the Battle of Flers-Courcelette. This weapon was very primitive at this stage and indeed for the rest of the war, though later versions were a vast improvement on the Mark I.

The original scheme was dubbed the 'Caterpillar Project'. First 'Little Willie' was born, driven by a Daimler engine and running on Bullock tracks from America. Its shape was simply an oblong box sitting on the tracks, but later 'Big Willie' came along, with the tracks going round the edge of a lozenge shaped steel body. The shape and basic design was settled but a name for the new machine was required. Eventually, partly to hide its true role and perhaps because it was an easy word, 'tank' was selected. Demonstrations were arranged; the

King, Lord Kitchener, Lloyd George and many others were impressed, though some of the generals were (not without reason) sceptical. In the spring of 1916 a new tank force came into being known as the Armoured Car Section of the Motor Machine Gun Service. In August 1916 the first, primitive, Mk I tanks were brought to France. During the battle of Flers the tank performed reasonably well, though it was mechanical unreliable. It was unwieldly and slow, and it needed to halt to turn. Conditions inside for the crew were appalling; its armour splintered on the inside when hit and its gun was extremely limited and its vulnerability to field guns soon became apparent. Whatever the criticisms that might be levelled against it, Haig, already an enthusiast, was further persuaded and called for huge deliveries of the new weapon.

Elles was appointed Brigadier General commanding the tank battalions. In July 1917 it became the Tank Corps. Prior to that a depot of the Heavy Section Machine Gun Corps, as the tank crews were then labelled, was established in a forty acre site at Bermicourt, near St Pol, west of Arras.

Tanks went into action east of Arras in 1917 where they put up a very mixed performance, and the Australians, for one, had good reason to be deeply suspicious of them. They also had little success when attacking alongside them in the Ypres Salient. The conditions were very difficult for such a vehicle. The tanks reputation suffered badly – more than 200 were lost there and much of the infantry wanted nothing to do with them. The Australians and the 51st ((Highland)) Division, for example, would sooner go into battle without their support. By the time of Cambrai, the Mk IV tank was available. There were two types, a 'Male' and a 'Female'.

The male was 26'5" long, 13'6" wide, 8'2" high at the top of the tracks, 28 tons in weight with a 'spanning' capability of ten feet. It was constructed with armour plate, 12mm thick, powered by a six cylinder Daimler petrol engine. It was armed with two good ex-Naval Hotchkiss 6 pounder guns, with a modern vertical dropping breech block which gave a quick rate of fire. The barrels were shortened and mounted in sponsons, one on each side of the tank; it also carried three Lewis guns. Its maximum speed over 'good going' was 3.7 mph, with an average of 2 mph; but it was much less over battlefield conditions. It carried 70 gallons of fuel, used about two gallons per mile and had a radius of action of 15 miles. The crew consisted, generally, of one officer and seven other ranks. The 'Female' was 10'6" wide, weighed 27 tons and carried five Lewis guns.

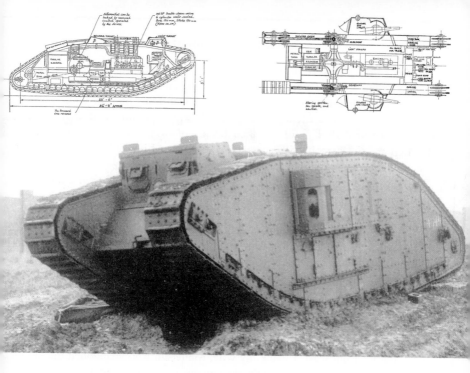

To work the tank was extremely difficult. It took three men to turn the long cranked handle to start it. Changing gear was a nightmare: each track was independent and had its own gear man and the tank had to stop before a new gear could be selected. Thus it moved in a series of slow zig-zags, making it very vulnerable. The conditions inside the tank were awful: hot, fume-filled with, in action, shards of metal stripped off by the impact of bullets and shrapnel, flying around. To talk was practically impossible due to the infernal noise. In fact three to four hours in the awful conditions was as much as a man could stand; they had to clear the tank before they fainted or were sick. Because of the petrol driven engine most of the fatal casualties among crews were caused by incineration. Observation from the tank was very limited as its periscopes were almost useless. The exit doors were small and had to remain closed in action. Getting out under battle conditions was extremely difficult. It was not fully appreciated by many at the time but the crews, all volunteers, were heroes. They were well aware of the limitations of their machines and the dangers that they posed.

Despite all this, Brigadier General Hugh Elles and his enthusiastic team believed implicitly in the new weapon, as did the crews. They were, one and all, convinced of the vital contribution it could make to winning the war.

Acknowledgements

Firstly I must thank Nigel Cave, who suggested that I should have a look at Flesquières and write its story; he then turned my labours into a readable volume. Monsieur Philippe Gorczynski of Cambrai and Jean-Luc Gibot of Gouzeaucourt, both researchers and writers on the First World War, provided indispensable assistance; particularly helpful was their book, *Following the Tanks at Cambrai*, a beautifully produced, mapped, researched and illustrated book. The photographs of 'then' in this book are mainly from their photographic library.

I would like to thank many of the Regimental Museums and their curators for their assistance, in particular Kate Thaxton for the wealth of information about the Royal Norfolk Regiment.

My grateful thanks go once again to the Commonwealth War Graves Commission, Maidenhead, which unfailingly provided registers of the Commonwealth War Cemeteries, so essential for the Tours Section of this book.

I owe much to the 'valiant' Wilkinson family at Pen & Sword, who really do all the hard work in putting my books together.

My thanks, of course, to the many French villagers who allowed me onto their land and willingly gave me all the information about events on their land in the time of their grandparents that they could.

Last, but far from least, I thank my wife, Mauveen, who abandoned the dining room and the small bedroom to all the documents, war diaries, computer print outs, etc. for seven months; and who accompanied me, once again, in the cold month of March, to test the battlefield tours. She has said, 'I'm not going again', for the last twenty-five years; but still she comes.

Advice To Tourers

The battle area is about eighty miles south-east of Calais. It is easily reached by the A26 autoroute. At Arras there is a junction with the A1, which will take you to Bapaume and the Somme. From there a very good and straight road, the N30, connects with Cambrai, about seventeen miles to the east. However, it is recommended you keep to the A26, for the accommodation in Cambrai is very extensive, being a larger town. There is a selection of available accommodation listed below. The battlefields in this volume are along and south of the N30, starting roughly half way between Bapaume and Cambrai and within a seven mile west and south arc of the ridge-top village of Flesquières. The area is off the beaten track for most visitors to the Western Front yet it was of great importance. Not only is there the unknowable impact on the course of the war of a complete victory at Cambrai, but there was also important fighting here in March 1918 and in the final Advance to Victory. The land and villages we will see were fought over in 1917 and 1918 on four occasions. Individual sites will be visited more than once to take account of these actions.

The tours can be taken in any order. Each could take a full day, but if time is at a premium they can be 'telescoped'. The distance from Cambrai to the start of each tour is about eleven miles.

There are many shops and supermarkets in Cambrai and Bapaume and a number of villages have a shop. You should ensure your car's fuel tank is filled before setting out. It is suggested that you take a picnic with you; restaurants are few on the battlefields and shops close promptly at midday. Plastic plates, cutlery, glasses and a cork screw will doubtless be useful.

Although the guide is well mapped it is recommended that you purchase the two maps of the relevant IGN (equivalent to the Ordnance Survey) Series Bleu. These are the 1:25,000, 2507 O, Croisilles and 2507 E Cambrai (Ouest) Marcoing. These are reasonably easy to obtain in bookshops and some newsagents in France; and also from the IGN web site on the internet. These maps cover the area of the tours.

The land in the five tours has been almost entirely cleared of war debris, unexploded shells, grenades, etc.; but if you should come across anything then LEAVE WELL ALONE. Old munitions can still be (indeed are) lethal.

Remember that this is farming land so please respect the crops and do not leave your car blocking access to farmers' lands and buildings. The land is their livelihood; under no circumstances go walking through planted fields. This might seem obvious, but on too many occasions people have ignored the basic courtesies of the countryside. Keep to the edge of fields (although after harvest this is not so important) and seek permission where possible. The farmers do not see many pilgrims to the battlefields and, in my experience, without exception are always helpful and will show you things and places you would otherwise never see. Be very alert to the dangers presented by hunters during the season, particularly at week ends.

Do not forget all the essentials for motorists: adequate insurance, breakdown assistance, a small medical kit, warning triangles and spare bulbs, almost all of which are compulsory in France. Ensure that your passport is current, that you bring the E111 medical form, obtainable from your Post Office, good boots and waterproofs, a camera, sufficient spare film and a notebook to keep a record of what you have photographed.

There are twenty-four cemeteries included in the tours. However, there are many more relevant to this story. Among the twenty-four cemeteries there are approximately 9,000 graves, of which 2,000 are 'unknown'. In four of the 'Front Line' cemeteries the percentage of 'unknown' graves is high, more than fifty per cent in one. In the largest burial ground, on the far edge of the 'arc' near Ytres, where there were a number of Casualty Clearing Stations, out of 1,838 graves only 22 are 'unknown'.

Before starting out, if you wish to know where any particular man is buried, then the Commonwealth War Graves Commission's office at 2 Marlow Road, Maidenhead , Berks, SL6 7FX, Tel: 01628 634221 or E mail: casualty.enq@cwgc.org, will willingly help. In addition you can visit the CWGC's excellent web site, and try and locate the individual memorial from that.

Accomodation

The tours have been designed on the assumption that you are staying in or near Cambrai. However if you are combining a visit with one to the Somme Region, then one or two possibilities there have been included. For all fax and telephone numbers, calling from outside France, prefix the number with 0033 3:

1. Hotel Beatus, five hundred yards from the old Paris Gate,   718, Avenue de Paris, 59400 Cambrai. Tel: 27.81.45.70. Fax: 27.78.00.83. The owner, M. Philippe Gorczynski is most helpful.
2. Hotel Ibis, Route de Bapaume, 59400 Fontaine, Tel 13.27.82.99.88. Fax: 27.82.99.88.
3. Hotel Campanile, Route de Bapaume. Tel:27.81.62.00. Fax: 27.83.07.87
4. Hotel de la Poste, 58 avenue de la Victoire, Tel:27.78.09.59 Fax: 27.83.95.08

There are many others, the addresses of which can be obtained from the Office de Tourisme, Cambrai.

Accommodation on the Somme:
1. Avril Williams Guest House, 10 Rue Delattre, Auchonvillers 80560, Tel: 33.322.76.23.66. She is British.
2. Julie Renshaw, Les Galets, Auchonvillers 80560, Tel: 33.422.76.28.79. She is British.
3. Hotel de la Paix, Bapaume 62450, Tel:-33.321.07.11.03

Accommodation on the Battlefield:
1. Ferme des Ecarts, Les Rue de Vignes, Masnières 59241 Tel:-33.327.37.51.00
2. La Ferme de Bonavis, Carrefour RN44 et D917, Banteux 59266, Tel:- 33.327.78.55.08

MAPS   Page

Page   **Tour Maps**

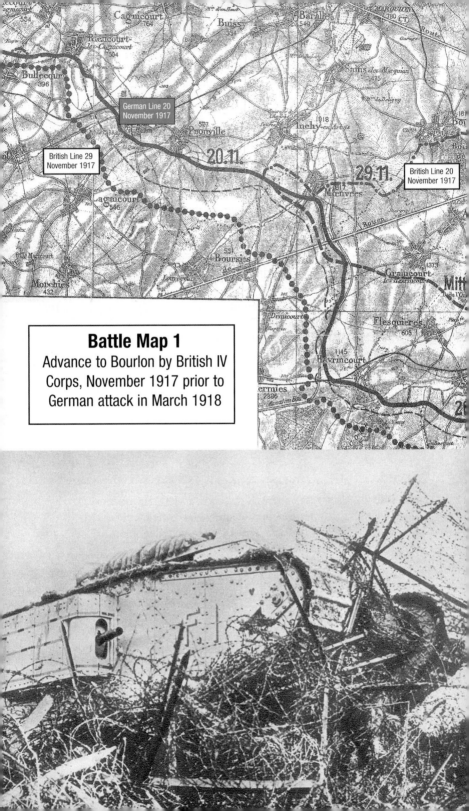

Battle Map 1

Advance to Bourlon by British IV Corps, November 1917 prior to German attack in March 1918

German Line 20 November 1917

British Line 29 November 1917

British Line 20 November 1917

Chapter One

SETTING THE SCENE

In the late Spring of 1917 Ludendorff was reasonably content with the progress of the war. The Russians had begun their revolution and the Eastern Front had collapsed and soon he would have battle hardened divisions available from there to fight in the west. The French were struggling to recover their morale and strength after the debacle of the Chemin des Dames offensive. The British were held in the west; his men had successfully withdrawn to their new positions well east of the Somme fighting of 1916. His men had fought a well executed fighting retreat, inflicting many casualties as they went eastwards; they destroyed villages, houses, churches, bridges, culverts, orchards, woods, blocking roads and railway tracks, obliterating crops, and poisoning wells in the arid plain east of Bapaume. Nothing would remain west of his Siegfried Stellung to offer succour to the advancing British. A cold, hard man he thought nothing of this scorched earth policy, but his local Army Commander, Prince Rupprecht of Bavaria, was so appalled at the destruction his men were ordered to cause that he offered to resign.

Ludendorff could now rebuild his army for the final onslaught against the Allies and win the war or, at the very least, create an atmosphere after the Allies inevitably huge losses in men and territory that they would sue for peace. He discounted the

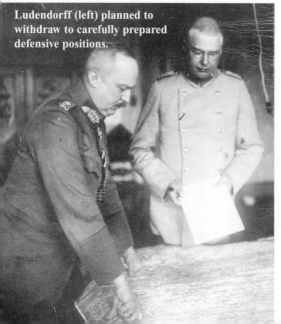

Ludendorff (left) planned to withdraw to carefully prepared defensive positions.

Prince Rupprecht of Bavaria was appalled at the planned devastation of the land and threatened to resigned.

Americans (who entered the war in April 1917), considering that they would be in no condition to provide the necessary manpower and experience before the crucial moment.

In May 1917, General Sir Henry Rawlinson's Fourth Army, following the German's withdrawal, at a heavy cost in casualties, arrived in front of the ten mile long section of the Hindenburg Line before Cambrai. It was the 42nd (East Lancs) Division TF that came to Havrincourt Wood and the banks of the Canal du Nord, the 'Dry Ditch'. The Germans had cut down two hundred acres of the trees in the north-west part of the wood, bordering the curve of the canal, to give them a better view of the British lines from Havrincourt. They had left the felled timber on the ground to prevent an easy passage for the British. The Lancashire Territorials' task was to patrol up to and into the enemy's line to keep him off balance and to find out just how impenetrable the barbed wire and trench system actually was. This patrolling was mutual, the enemy making similar forays into the British lines; an activity which would go on for four or five months. As Sergeant Sugden of the 10/Manchesters reported, 'the wood (Havrincourt) was alive with Germans'. The British soon discovered the strength of the German defences and the formidable power of the enemy artillery, the batteries of which were close behind the Line's support system, with every cross road and British position registered.

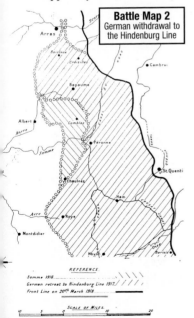

Battle Map 2
German withdrawal to the Hindenburg Line

REFERENCE.
Somme 1916
German retreat to Hindenburg Line 1917
Front Line on 20th March 1918

SCALE OF MILES.

The long lines of East Lancashire graves in the cemeteries of the villages two and three miles to the west, Neuville – Bourjonval, Ruyaulcourt, Bertincourt and Ytres bear witness to this. On 8 July the division went north with the Fourth Army to the dreaded Ypres Salient. Now the Third Army of General the Hon. Sir Julian Byng, 'the man who, as Canadian Corps commander masterminded the capture of Vimy Ridge in April 1917', arrived.

On 24 April Haig, the British Commander in Chief, met his French counterpart, Robert Nivelle. Amongst other matters, a proposal for an attack on the Cambrai front was discussed. It would be a joint attack with the French in the south at St Quentin and the

British at Havrincourt. The next day Haig directed Generals Sir Henry Rawlinson and Sir Hubert Gough, commanding the Fourth and Fifth Armies respectively, to prepare plans for breaking into the Hindenburg Line at Havrincourt, 'and to occupy the Havrincourt-Flesquières Ridge'. Haig was well aware of Cambrai's importance, offering the possibility of getting behind the Germans in the north.

The plan was not submitted until 19 June and General Headquarters promptly began some preliminary preparations. Earlier, Nivelle had been replaced as Commander in Chief of the French Forces by General Philippe Pétain; in May Haig told him that he had in mind a two pronged attack on the Hindenburg Line with the French Army. However, he was about to embark on the Third Battle of Ypres; northern Flanders was always of paramount importance to him as he was utterly convinced of its strategic significance. Therefore he could not commit to anything elsewhere; he simply did not have the manpower to do it.

It was now left to Byng's Third Army to prepare for a possible attack in the area at some undetermined date. A number of his senior officers

General Rawlinson (Fourth Army), General Byng (Third Army), Field Marshal Sir Douglas Haig and General Horne (First Army).

welcomed the proposal but two would have an outstanding influence. One was the commander of the fledgling Tank Corps in France, Brigadier General Hugh Elles; the other was Brigadier General HH Tudor, commanding the artillery in the 9th (Scottish) Division, part of Lieutenant General Woollcombe's IV Corps. On 4 August 1917 Elles secured the interest of Brigadier General JH Davidson, Chief of the Operations Section at GHQ, in his ideas; the following day Colonel J Hardress-Lloyd, one of Elles's brigade commanders, took the scheme to Byng. Byng agreed that if the attack on Cambrai did take place he would incorporate some tank action. At this time all thoughts and eyes were on the battle at Ypres, now in full swing.

Brigadier General Tudor conceived the plan of a surprise attack at Cambrai as a diversion from the 'slogging match' in the north. He had studied the success achieved by the German artillery expert Colonel Bruchmüller who had earlier successfully planned an accurate bombardment without previous artillery registration. It fell only a few hours before the infantry attack, its shock achieving victory.

The basis of the plan was that the tanks would crush the wire for the infantry; simultaneously the barrage would fall on selected targets as the infantry advanced, eliminating the need for a prolonged early barrage that often did not cut the wire sufficiently and also alerted the enemy defenders. This is what had happened in the week long barrage at the beginning of the Somme offensive. His plan intended particularly to remove the threat from German batteries, so called counter-battery fire.

Within his scheme were an advance to the Flesquières Ridge and a smaller operation to the north. The seizure of Cambrai was not then envisaged.

Things at this high level take time, the winter was only three months away and despite all the thinking and planning it was not until the middle of September when plans begun to firm up. During the summer months Elles had scoured battlefields for disabled tanks, bringing them into the tank workshops at Bermicourt to refurbish and modify them. He also received new tanks from England, assembling a growing force of the latest Mk IV model. Recruiting was strong, many men, particularly gunners, being attracted to the new arm and training was advanced. He knew that sooner or later his Tank Corps would be called upon and he was determined to succeed.

Tudor was also hard at work and his task, when permitted to embark on it, was enormous. The artillery plan required 'map shooting', whereby every battery would be issued with an 'Artillery Board' on which was plotted ranges and directions of the targets, all calculated by trigonometry, fixed by sound ranging, air observation, 'flash spotting' and aerial photographs – a revolutionary change from the earlier days of the war and clear evidence of the adaptation of new technology. The characteristics of every gun, its calibration and its muzzle velocity as well as its individual idiosyncrasies had to be known accurately – every gun is different. Weather, pressure and meteorological information are vital. If all this could be achieved, then the guns could be hidden, and brought into the line at the last moment to deliver an accurate and stunning barrage on predetermined targets. The old fashioned style of a creeping barrage, behind which the infantry would advance at great cost, would not be employed. By no means were these new ideas, and today would seem an obvious tactic. However, previously it had been unachievable.

In the middle of September Haig reviewed his options and Cambrai came up again. It could hardly have gone away, so enthusiastic was Third Army. It was vital that the enemy should not get any suspicions about the possibility of an attack and secrecy was of paramount importance. Considering the size of the project, the movement of hundreds of tanks, guns, horses and more than 350,000 men, that its secret was maintained until a few hours before the attack began – when only a tiny fragment was leaked – was perhaps the main reason for its initial success. It was certainly one of the best kept secrets of the war up to then, but was a sign of the increased flexibility of the British army and an indication of things to come in 1918, in battles such as Le Hamel and the attack of 8th August 1918.

On 16 September Byng took his scheme to Haig. He asked for an extra 3,000 men for each of his five divisions and was promised all possible help. However, as yet no date or commitment could be given whilst the Ypres battle was in progress – soon to make very considerable progress during the Battle of the Menin Road.

Meanwhile Third Army continued with its work: repairs and essential engineering work had to take place regardless of any attack on Cambrai. Tens of thousands of gallons of water had to be brought forward; the nearest rivers were the Somme and the Ancre. Roads ruined by the enemy had to be reconstructed, bridges had to be rebuilt and railway lines reinstalled. Hundreds of lorries moved back and forth at night, without lights; by dawn all evidence of work done during the night was hidden.

On 13 October the Commander in Chief gave his approval for preliminary preparations to begin: if the offensive did not begin soon, whatever its size and objectives, winter would prevent it. On 26 October Byng held a conference with his staff and told them to go ahead, but no date was fixed. All of them knew it had to be within a month. Tudor's idea for unregistered shooting could now be put into effect; the surveying task was given to Major BFE Keeling, commanding 3rd Field Survey Company RE. He had only two assistants who would work night and day. The plan used more than 1,000 guns from 18 pounders (700 of them) to three 15″ railway mounted guns. Six hundred and seventy of the guns were brought in especially for the battle. None of these could yet be put into place; instead their intended location was marked out by pegs and the artillery boards prepared from these positions. The boards would give the gunners accurate target information at the time of hauling the guns into their prepared positions during hours of darkness.

Elles and his team were also hard at work. He had viewed the battlefield from various observation points. He was well aware of the deep and wide trenches that his tanks would have to cross. If a tank could not approach at right angles but went 'side on' the commander's and the steersmens' ability to see was extremely limited, and they could 'broach' and become stuck. He devised a system of attack to reduce this possibility and a fascine to fill the gap of the trench. All of the fighting tanks – and there would be 378 of them – would carry on their front a great roll of brushwood, 4′ 6″ in diameter, 10″ long and weighing almost two tons. These further reduced the already limited vision. Each roll would be held together by chain, two tanks being

Tanks with the huge bundles fascines already in place. The fascines were a method devised for assisting tanks to cross trenches in the forthcoming attack. They would be dropped into the enemy trench and act as a bridge.

involved to pull it tight before it was secured.

Great Britain was scoured for this chain. 12,000 feet of it was brought to Bermicourt where a 1,000 men of the 51st Chinese Labour Company would make 400 fascines. In addition they made more than a 100 wooden sledges, each capable of carrying two tons of supplies, each to be towed, three at a time, by thirty old tanks They would carry petrol, oil, water and ammunition. Elles was also concerned about the Grand Ravine, a marked feature that ran below Flesquières Ridge; in fact it was not filled with water, as was feared, and it proved to be only a minor obstacle. He hoped to be able to put more than 400 tanks into action.

The fighting around Ypres which had started so well at the beginning of October had now stalled, and it was only a matter of time before the offensive was closed down. The time for the Cambrai offensive was drawing closer when the Germans and their Austrian allies struck a telling blow in Italy.

On 4 October the Austro-Hungarian Army, under the direction of the Germans and stiffened by six of their divisions, attacked on the Isonzo River in the mountains of north east Italy. The Italian line was broken and the rout of their Sixth Army took place. In the fifty mile withdrawal, which would last eighteen days, the Italians lost 650,000 men out of 1,400,000 combatants and 3,000 guns. It appeared that the total collapse of Italy might be imminent and help from Pétain and Haig was imperative. The War Cabinet told Haig to supply at once for Italy two divisions from the Western Front, with more to follow, six batteries of heavy artillery, two air squadrons. The force was to be commanded by General Sir Hubert Plumer, then General Officer Commanding (GOC) Second Army at Ypres. Three days later he was told that further demands were likely to be made. Lieutenant General Sir Launcelot Kiggell, Haig's Chief of Staff, was sent to London to explain to the War Cabinet how the demands for Italy would affect prospects for the operations in France. His arguments made no impression, particularly on the Prime Minister, Lloyd George, who was no friend of Haig.

Haig's view was that renewed attacks in the west would be the quickest and surest way of relieving the Italians. He believed that unless that took place, thus attracting experienced German divisions now released from the quiescent Russian Front, Ludendorff would direct them to Italy or possibly toward the weakened French Army. Haig told his Chief of Staff to inform London that, with the exception of the artillery battle, the Ypres offensive would cease on 13

November. He hoped thereby to persuade the Germans that operations were still underway, and thus prevent the them from transfering troops away to other fronts. He also wrote to Sir William Robertson, the Chief of the Imperial General Staff, explaining this. In addition, he would rapidly stop all operations at Cambrai if he could see it was not going to be a success.

In the event the reinforcements for Italy were not required on a large scale. The Italian Army, without the active intervention of the British or the French, brought the Central Powers' offensive to a halt at the lower Piave. British troops remained for the rest of the war in Italy, and under their commander, the Earl of Cavan, played an important role in the last days of the war there, a largely neglected part of the British Army's Great War campaign.

The plan for the Battle of Cambrai was now put into effect. The date for it to commence, Tuesday 20 November, was not divulged until a few days before. All concerned realised that the time scale was extremely short and from the outset Haig had told Byng he would stop the offensive after 48 hours – or even earlier – if the general situation did not justify its continuance. The objectives were: to break the enemy's defences with the help of tanks; to capture Cambrai (by encirclement), to take Bourlon Wood and the crossings of the Sensée, more than five miles north of Cambrai, and to exploit the success by advancing north-eastwards, rolling up the German lines from the south. By any standards it was an ambitious plan.

The critical points were to secure the bridges over the St Quentin Canal to permit the cavalry to sweep north, isolating Cambrai from potential German reinforcements, to secure the Flesquières Ridge, thereby allowing the capture of Bourlon. The capture of the latter would give the British control of the western gateway of Cambrai and domination of the northern plain to the Sensée River. All was to be done on the same day. These objectives were vital to success. If they were not accomplished within forty-eight hours, then the whole enterprise would be in jeopardy.

The attack would be on a 10,000 yard front. The infantry and tanks would advance for more than 5,000 yards to the objectives at the Canal and Flesquières Ridge; with a similar distance to go to the final objectives. Lieutenant General Kavanagh's Cavalry Corps was ready to come through the infantry to achieve the ultimate line, a vision that the cavalrymen had dreamt of, not least the Commander in Chief. The Third Army would have nineteen divisions in total but on the first, crucial, day only the 6th, 12th, 20th and 29th from Lieutenant General

Sir William Pulteney's III Corps and the 36th, 51st, 56th and 62nd from Lieutenant General Sir Charles Woollcombe's IV Corps would play an active part.

The four divisions from III Corps would break through the Hindenburg Line, heading north-east through La Vacquerie. Three divisions were to take bridges across the St Quentin Canal, and one, Major General Marden's 6th, would advance closer to the eastern edge of the Flesquières Ridge. IV Corps would head north, the divisions positioned from south to north in the order 51st (heading for Flesquières), 62nd (Havrincourt), 36th and 56th.

Haig informed General Pétain on 1 November of the projected operation; plans were made for the French to assist with two cavalry and three infantry divisions which would strike south once a gap in the German line at the St Quentin Canal had been made. The bridges at Crèvecoeur were, therefore, essential.

Training and the assembly of the huge mountain of supplies needed could now begin. How this was achieved without the alert enemy being aware of what was to fall on them was a wonder of deception and desperately hard work. Everything brought forward had to be hidden, amongst which were a million rounds of artillery ammunition, most of it within a 1,000 yards of the front of the Hindenburg Line. Thirty thousand of the rounds were enormous shells for the 8″, 9.2″, 12″ and 15″ howitzers. Consider the numbers of lorries required, all travelling at night, slowly in low gear to reduce their noise, and with lights in the dark November nights forbidden. In addition there were needed millions of small arms and machine gun rounds, trench mortar bombs, hand grenades, barbed wire, trench ladders and bridges: all the accoutrements of war, not to mention food for the men and fodder for the horses and mules. The Tank Corps alone needed 36 trains to bring it forward. Not a small part of its requirements were reserves for each of its three brigades: 30,000 gallons of petrol, 5,000 lbs of grease, 2,500 gallons of vacuum lubricating oil, 5,000 gallons of steam cylinder thick oil (this liquid alone required two trains); 100,000 rounds of 6 pounder ammunition; and some millions of Lewis gun rounds. They would need 50,000 gallons in the tanks at the start of the operation. Dumps were established at railheads, three to five miles behind the line: at Ytres, Ruyaulcourt and Tincourt and elsewhere as far back as Bapaume. 100,000 square yards of camouflage netting were needed for the divisions of III Corps alone; even more for the IVth. The supply and backup services, from such arms as the Army Service Corps, the Royal Army Medical Corps and the Royal

Engineers, generally get but a small mention in battles. Their work here was notable, as was that of the quartermasters at all levels. Medical facilities were bolstered; for example there were Main Dressing Stations for III Corps at Fins, three miles south of the Bonavis Ridge, three for IV Corps at Ruyaulcourt, Lebucquière and Beugny and two Casualty Clearing Stations at Ytres, the 21st and the 48th, close to the Rocquigny-Equancourt road.

The four divisions of cavalry, which in the event would play a very small part as cavalry, all came forward to positions close to the Bonavis Ridge at the southern edge of the bowl. Their thousands of horses and men all had to be hidden from German air observation, whilst watering and feeding their animals was a great task (not to mention the much larger number of horses and mules required to haul guns and supplies).

III Brigade of the Royal Flying Corps was reinforced until it had 289 planes, fighters, bombers and reconnaissance aircraft. They would attack the German airfields around Cambrai and at dawn, as the attack began, would fly low over the front line, obscuring the noise of the tanks starting up and machine gunning and bombing the German trenches.

Elles had devised a particular method of attack. Tanks would be in units of three. Having penetrated the wire, the first tank would turn left down the first trench, spraying the occupants with its machine guns. The next two would use the track made by the first, one dropping its

This picture gives some idea of the huge quantity of ammunition required for an offensive. The presence of the horse drawn limber illustrates the dependence on muscle power – horse and human.

British infantry training to attack with tank support.

fascine into the trench and then crossing it and turning left, the other
crossing the trench and advancing to the support trench and dropping
its fascine into that. There would be one tank, it was hoped, for every
hundred yards of attack front. The infantry would follow in single file
by sections, keeping close. Subsequently the specially equipped tanks
would drag the wire away for the benefit of the cavalry. Once through
the wire the infantry would mop up the trenches, forming stops in
them, capturing Germans, consolidating positions and eliminating
enemy machine gun posts and any artillery. The infantry's paramount
task was to eliminate enemy resistance, thus protecting the tank from
attack.

Training in these methods began in early November when battalions
in turn were withdrawn from the line. The 62nd and the 51st Divisions
went to Wailly, just south-west of Arras, the 6th to Beaufort, six miles
further west. Each division only had ten days for the training, and
battalions two days each before they returned to the trenches,
patrolling and taking casualties. Full scale models of their part of the
Hindenburg Line were laid out. To help in gaining their confidence,
infantry were invited to construct any form of trench or obstruction to
show the ease with which a tank could deal with it. The tank
commanders were well aware of many of the infantrymen's lack of
confidence in them.

During the second week of November Haig watched this training,
underlining the essential support of rifle and Lewis Gun that the tanks
would need. IV Corps Headquarters in Villers-au-Flos issued
instructions that should a tank breakdown then the infantry must
swerve and keep well clear of the obvious target. Not all divisional
commanders were convinced. Major General Harper, commanding the
51st, devised a system of his own which forbade the infantry to follow

the tanks in section files. His men would advance in two ranks and were told to avoid fire directed at the tanks by never coming closer than one hundred yards of the machines. The men were instructed not cross any trench until it had been engaged by the tanks. It was a controversial decision, one that has exercised military historians ever since; but it probably was not as fatal to his part of the attack as was hitherto thought. Major General Braithwaite also had little confidence in the ability of the tanks and believed that it was impossible for sections or platoons to follow a specific tank; the 62nd Division did not practise close affiliation either.

Elles would be able to put into the attack: 378 fighting tanks in nine battalions; 54 supply tanks, 32 for wire pulling and two carrying bridges. Each battalion would have a wireless tank and so there would be a total of 476 tanks. There would be no tank concentration, movement of artillery or attacking infantry into their lying up positions in the battle area until three days before 'Z' day. It was estimated that tanks could not approach their final positions, less than a 1,000 yards from the jumping off line, without the enemy hearing them. This determined the start lines of the battle.

General von der Marwitz.

On the other side of the line, the German forces were part of General von der Marwitz's Second Army, on the left of Crown Prince

A new breed of German infantryman – the stormtrooper. An inspection is being carried out.

Rupprecht's Group of Armies. The two divisions facing the attack at Havrincourt and Flesquières were the 20th Landwehr and the 54th. From Havrincourt north to a mile above the Cambrai-Bapaume road was Lieutenant General Freiherr von Hanstein's 20th Landwehr Division, a second line formation, thinly spread for about six miles, which had arrived only eight days earlier. Below it, from Havrincourt to six miles south of La Vacquerie, was Lieutenant General Freiherr von Watter's 54th Division. It was battle hardened but badly depleted and weary, having been brought down from Ypres in August to rest in the 'Flanders Sanatorium'. Its artillery consisted of three howitzer and six field gun batteries, 34 guns, plus one medium battery of 5.9s. It had three other batteries of captured pieces, one Russian, one French, one Belgian. There was also a battery of heavy mortars. It was very short of ammunition but was unconcerned, convinced of the security of the Siegfried Stellung and of the thought that the usual prolonged British artillery bombardment would give ample time to organise an appropriate defence. The 20th Landwehr was scheduled to be relieved on 25 November by Major General Havenstein's 107th Division, an experienced formation from the Russian Front. With it would come more artillery batteries, some of which began to take up positions with the 54th on the 18th. A warning order had been issued from the Crown Prince's HQ that an attack was anticipated in the Havrincourt sector and tanks might be used. A lengthy preliminary bombardment was expected.

On the 18th, Major Hofmeister's 84th Infantry Regiment was in the Ribécourt area. That night the Germans were ordered to carry out a prisoner capturing sortie at Trescault, a ridge top village just inside the British Line. Lieutenant Hegermann, commanding the raid, captured a sergeant and five men of an Irish Regiment of the 36th (Ulster) Division. His commander was surprised when, under questioning, he was told that a large attack was being prepared for the 20th on Havrincourt and that camouflaged tanks had been seen in the woods. The information was not believed; he had seen the poor performance of the tanks at Ypres and he felt that the British would not be so stupid as to try an attack on the strongest part of the Siegfried Stellung. He simply sent the prisoners, with a report, back to Army Group Headquarters. Nevertheless at headquarters other things had been

reported, a lot of aircraft activity, large traffic movements and a fragment of a telephone message, 'Tuesday, Flanders', had been heard. Once again the information was passed on to the Second Army Headquarters. But an assault from Trescault on Havrincourt and Flesquières was considered unlikely, so no special measures were taken. On the 19th it was seen that traffic and movement on the British side had still further increased; local commanders began to put their battalions on a state of alert.

In the dark hours of the 20th, just before dawn, they saw British infantry cutting their own wire. Obviously, if nothing else, a large scale raid was in the offing and von Watter, in his HQ in the chateau at Havrincourt, ordered an artillery bombardment on the British Line. It lasted no more than half an hour; unusually, and disturbingly, the British artillery did not respond.

The British were lucky with the weather in their preparations; it was a typical November: dull, misty and with rain helping to screen preparations. Where to hide Byng's massive force had been a problem, particularly the tanks. Places had to be found amongst the ruined buildings of villages such as Metz, Ytres, Neuville-Bourjonval, Ruyaulcourt and others. The woods, which were always shelled, had to be used, whilst the fallen and broken trees and their stumps provided a hazard to the machines. Shelter had to be made for the infantry amongst the ruins of villages and shacks were erected in woods such as Havrincourt, Velù, Dessart, Gouzeaucourt and others – as close as possible to the start line. Artillery and tanks were brought closer to the Army area from Arras and west of Bapaume and Pèronne, whilst the attacking infantry, who had been training with the tanks also came

The formidable barbed wire obstacles of the Hindenburg Line south-west of Flesquières.

forward. The whole of the Tank Corps entrained in thirty-six trains between the 15th and 18th, the tanks already bearing the fascines. Each tank carried its full complement of ammunition and two days rations for the eight man crew; the rations included a bottle of whiskey and rum, sustenance they would sorely need. The 670 guns were also moved forward as Major Keeling struggled to complete his task, each pegged out and camouflaged gun position gradually and secretly receiving its piece. In fact Keeling did not complete his last task, the positioning of a 9.2″ howitzer on the railway at Metz, vital to enfilade an important road, until two hours before Zero.

The German Defences

A German division had three regiments of infantry, usually of three battalions. The German defence scheme called for a lightly, but effectively, manned front line which would delay any attack long enough for counter-attack formations to be brought up to crush the offensive. There were two regiments of artillery, the 108th and the 213th, mainly equipped with 77mm field guns, to defend Flesquières Ridge. At the Havrincourt village end were Nos. 7, 8 and 9 batteries from the 213th and Nos. 2 and 8 from the 108th in and about Flesquières. They were short of ammunition.

The front, outpost, line of heavy gauge barbed wire on metal cruciforms crossed the 'Dry Ditch' from west to east, 600 yards above the blown bridge over the ninety foot deep gorge. This was closely followed by a well built trench on the eastern side of the canal bank. This outpost line then crossed the track from Havrincourt to Hermies at a great mine crater (Vesuvius) blown by the Germans and which was strongly manned. The line continued down the steep slope; 1,000 yards below was another, similarly manned, crater (Etna). Curving to the east the line continued south-easterly through the north east corner of Havrincourt Wood and then through Femy Wood, where the Germans had felled another 100 acres of trees to give them visibility into the British trenches. This would provide another difficult passage for tanks and artillery. The line then passed across the valley slope, 1,000 yards in front of Trescault and the British line. Paralleling it, crossing the 'Dry Ditch' a further 1,000 yards north, was the main band of the Siegfried Stellung, about 300 yards east of the dry canal, with three lines of barbed wire, 200 yards deep and with a further five rows behind it, all interlaced with strong, very wide trenches. It crossed the track to Hermies just east of Vesuvius, wrapped round the ridge top village of Havrincourt and then crossed the Grand Ravine and faced south 1,000 yards in front of Ribécourt. A Switch Line was situated 1,000 yards behind, equally strongly built. It ran from the north and flowed over the treeless plain in front of Flesquières and then went through this ridge top village before heading down the valley slope in a south-easterly direction, crossing the railway line 1,000 yards north of Ribécourt.

Thus in front of the British line, from the bend of the 'ditch' west of Havrincourt, crossing the Trescault Ridge close to the Grand Ravine, and then running west to east, facing the ridges of Havrincourt and Flesquières, was a front section of the Hindenburg Line 1,750 yards wide, consisting of fifteen rows of barbed wire even before the climb to Flesquières. There a further strongly defended line 300 yards deep protected the village.

Once that line was broken, to the north it was flat land stretching towards the main road and Bourlon Wood with defences round the intervening villages and hamlets.

The projected attack on the left of Flesquières Ridge would come out of the treeless Oxford Valley, situated between the two arms of Havrincourt Wood, and from there up the steep, open, bullet-swept incline to Havrincourt. On the right the attack would proceed from Trescault and down the valley side for 2,500 yards to the Grand

A section of German trench on the Hindenburg Line.

Ravine; and from there up the other side to Flesquières. Below the ridge, in the treeless valley, were two small woods, T Wood to the right of Havrincourt village, half way up the slope, and Triangle Wood, down towards the valley bottom and within the Hindenburg Line defence. No Man's Land had an average depth of 1,000 yards.

Manning the defences between Ribécourt and Havrincourt was Colonel von Wangenheim's 387th Infantry Regiment. On its left was Major Hermsdorff's 90th Reserve Regiment. On the right was Major Hofmeister's 84th and the 27th Reserve Regiment, commanded by Major Krebs. At the canal was the 384th Infantry Regiment. As the battle of the 20th progressed, infantry from Major General Havenstein's 107th Division were rushed up from Cambrai.

Captain Soltau of the 84th Regiment was defending Havrincourt village, based in the chateau. Von Watter had prudently evacuated the 54th Division's HQ to the chateau in La Folie Wood, a mile south of Fontaine Notre Dame; by the end of the first day, surprised by the weight and success of what he thought was a raid, he moved it back to Cambrai. All of this part of the battle area was his responsibility.

The British IV Corps Plan of Attack.
The Plan for the Artillery

On 'Z' day the barrage would open up on the outpost line at 6.20am. A number of field batteries were moved during the night to camouflaged positions close to the infantry's front line trenches along Hubert Road, which ran from the top left hand corner of Havrincourt Wood at the point where the trees had been felled to the south-east corner and E and D Battalions of the Tank Corps' laying up position. Any firing that took place then would be of the normal kind, such as had happened during the previous three months. Any retaliation to an enemy bombardment in the dark hours of the 19th/20th was forbidden to ensure surprise. The 670 extra guns were placed in position without alerting the enemy. Later prisoners were asked if they had heard the sounds of the arrival of guns or tanks; they had not. All they had heard was a tractor which had been towing two large howitzers in the distance. All of these new arrivals had been calibrated, and checked for the effect of barrel wear, before being brought into their camouflaged, pegged out positions.

The scheme was based on covering the whole attack with the minimum of forward movement. However, field batteries were given special routes to captured positions already selected for a further advance, with fascines being used to facilitate the passage of guns and limber wheels and the gunners were issued with wire cutters to improve the gaps to permit horse teams to pass. Heavy artillery would remain until the roads were adequate for their passage and the necessary ammunition. It was arranged in IV Corps that as soon as the Second Line had been breached some large guns and howitzers would take up positions in Boursies, some 2,000 yards west of the 'Dry Ditch', and would put down a heavy barrage on Bourlon, 7,500 yards away.

The RFC would spot for the artillery, there would also be balloons and artillery observers would quickly establish forward posts in the captured enemy positions. Some observers would move forward with the infantry to ensure close cooperation. The siege and heavy batteries would neutralise hostile guns, observation posts, main routes and billets and command posts. A smoke barrage would be required in various places, particularly on the Havrincourt-Flesquières Ridge. The high explosives barrage would not creep but lift from one trench line to the next as each was taken. That barrage, from field guns, 18 pounder and 4.5″ howitzers all firing instantaneous fused shells (new since the tail end of the Battle of the Somme), would be of high explosive and shrapnel. Truck-mounted anti-tank guns had to be spotted and dealt with immediately. Smoke would be fired from the outset, smothering the approaches to Havrincourt village and fired for forty minutes on a 2,000 yard length on the slopes of Flesquières. The continuance of this would depend on the wind and the infantry's needs. As it was expected the cavalry would soon join the battle a careful watch was to be made to ensure the lifting of the barrage. The Royal Engineers would be present to make bridges and ramps where required. It was calculated the rate of fire for the very heavy and medium guns would depend upon the circumstances. The field guns,

British 9.2 inch howitzers about to fire. This gun was one of the great work horses of the British army.

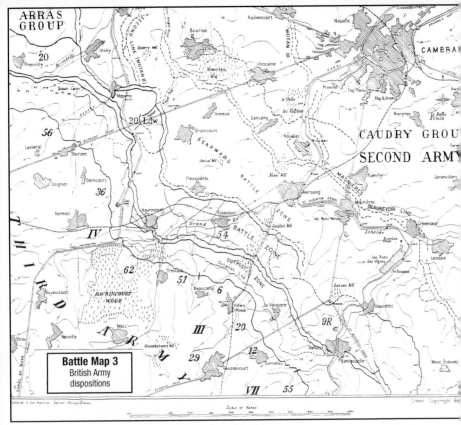

Battle Map 3
British Army
dispositions

18 pounders and light 4.5″ Howitzers, would fire four rounds per minute for periods of not more than ten minutes; on average the rate was to be two rounds per minute; whilst the 6″ howitzers fired one round every three minutes. The heavier guns, 8″ and 9.2″, would fire one round every five minutes. It was thought that the advance would be so certain and quick that this rate of fire would easily be adequate. However it was essential that the ammunition dumps should be maintained at not less than 100 rounds per field gun and 75 for the super heavies.

Of all the actions on that first day it was the barrage which had the most marked effect on the course of the battle. The shock of it stunned the German infantry.

The Plan for the Tanks

At the beginning of November, Elles had partially moved his Headquarters from Bermicourt into a battered former music hall in the ruined former front line town of Albert. His command was made up of three brigades, each with three battalions (given a letter from A to I) of three companies. Each of the twenty-seven companies was numbered from one to twenty-seven and was commanded by a major. All the tanks were lettered and numbered. They were given names starting with the battalion's letter, for example in the 1st Company of A Battalion, tank A1 was called *Armagh II*, A6 was *Ajax* and so on.

In the middle of November, Elles took his subordinate officers down to the level of company commander to the front line to view the battlefield. Many were amazed at its great depth of barbed wire and trenches. They also examined disembarkation ramps built by the Royal Engineers at the railway terminals, situated as far forward as possible. The railway men were mostly Americans of the 11th Engineer (Railway) Regiment. The brigade commanders would, in due course, place their headquarters at the railheads, along with those of their battalion commanders. Sites were selected for lying up places where the tanks would go just before the advance began.

Already the ubiquitous Major Frederick Hotblack and his reconnaissance teams were at work, searching for the best approach marches to the front line, walking through the dangerous Havrincourt Wood, the worst of all the terrain that had to be crossed. They made maps and noted references for the eventual use of the tank commanders.

Of the 378 fighting tanks, approximately half were Female, carrying only six Lewis Guns. These were spread out between battalions which were each divided into four sections of four tanks, with battalions having an equal share of the 54 supply tanks and the 32 wire pullers. The remaining tanks were made up of an assortment of bridging and wireless vehicles, along with a solitary transporter tank.

Once unloaded at the ramps the tanks would move very slowly and quietly into their lying up positions. In all this night time movement, involving many trains, lorries and men, there was only one accident, near Ytres. In the dark a train collided with a lorry, derailing the last transporter wagon. Its tank fell off and, crushing the lorry, killed the two men inside it.

Major F E Hotblack.

The camouflaged hiding places were on a ten mile arc, from Bertincourt, 5,000 yards west of Havrincourt Wood, down through Fins to Heudecourt, 5,000 yards below Gonnelieu on the Bonavis Ridge, the southern end of Byng's attack.

In the area covered by this book it was decided that Lieutenant Colonel E.B. Hankey's 'G' Battalion of 1 Brigade would attack on the left, up the Havrincourt-Flesquières Ridge, supporting the 62nd (2nd West Riding) Division. On its right Lieutenant Colonel W.F. Kyngdon's 'D' Battalion would lead the 51st (Highland)) Division. 'E' Battalion (Lieutenant Colonel Burnett) would be on the right of 'D', and also with the Highlanders. Further over, Lieutenant Colonel C. Willoughby's 'H' Battalion (II Brigade) would go for Ribécourt and the eastern end of Flesquières Ridge in support of 71 Brigade of the 6th Division.

It was estimated that after the ridge had been taken the two divisions of IV Corps, despite enemy action, ditchings and mechanical breakdowns, would have at least half, sixty, of the tanks with which they had started out, plus another twenty from 71 Brigade's attack These would be refuelled and topped up with ammunition by the tanks towing sledges. It would not go to plan.

On top of the other difficulties, the crews had little experience of being shut up inside their machines under heavy fire for long periods. By the end of the day those who survived were utterly exhausted.

Before dawn on the 18th all battalions were in their lying up positions, well hidden with camouflage netting. G Battalion was in the bottom left hand corner of Havrincourt Wood, close to the road from Ruyaulcourt to Metz en Couture. D and E Battalions were in the opposite, bottom right hand, corner where the wood crossed the road from Metz to Trescault. H, the other Battalion involved with Flesquières Ridge, was hidden in Dessart Wood, two miles south of Metz, it had almost four miles to go to its jumping off place. There was no smoking, no lights and all the crews' duties had to be performed with the utmost quietness.

Immediately it went dark in the drizzle of the afternoon of the 19th the tanks started up and, with engines practically only ticking over, went forward. In front of each was its tank commander, almost all of whom were second lieutenants. Leading them were their company commanders, all of them majors. Unwinding a two inch wide strip of black tape with a white line running down the middle, men from Hotblack's reconnaissance team walked forward, locating the best routes they had already found. Tanks followed, guided by their officers. This was a very dangerous task, as the ground was full of obstacles: barbed wire, trenches, fallen trees, stumps – and it was pitch dark. Some of the men walking in front were caught up in the wire and, unseen by the drivers, killed. In front of them, where possible, infantrymen helped by filling in some trenches, but the advance was painfully slow, no more than a few hundred yards in an hour.

G Battalion had the most difficult time, having to cross the centre of the wood to get to Oxford Valley. The forming up line for the attack was based on the assumption that to get nearer to the front line than 1,000 yards would be too close, as the enemy would easily hear them. The intention was to arrive two or three hours before zero hour, which for the tanks was 6 am. The tanks were kept running quietly to keep the engines and crews warm, the company commanders staying alongside them. Some of these men would go into battle in one of their company's tanks, though with its complement of eight men it was already crowded.

When *Hilda* (H1 a male tank commanded by Second Lieutenant TH de B Leach) was warming up at the start line on Trescault Ridge near Beaucamp, the commander was surprised to hear a tap on the door. On opening it he saw Brigadier General Hugh Elles smoking his pipe, carrying the Tank Corps flag he had designed fastened to an ash stick. 'Five minutes to go,' he said, 'your tank is the centre of the whole line and I'm coming with you.' He had started a tradition for the Tank Corps which would never die, a commander leading his men into battle, his head out of the hatch, flying his regimental colour. Elles had also, on the eve of battle, written a stirring message to his men, Special Order No. 6.

Tomorrow the Tank Corps will have the chance for which it has been waiting for many months, to operate on good ground in the van of the battle. All that hard work and ingenuity can achieve has been done in the way of preparation. It remains for unit commanders and for tank crews to complete the work by judgement and pluck in the battle itself. In the light of past experience I leave the good name of the Corps with great confidence in their hands. I propose leading the attack of the centre Division.

It was signed, simply, Hugh Elles.

The message had been read out that evening by the commanders to their crews, one that would always be remembered and quoted.

At 6.10am all the tanks closed up and moved forward for the biggest attack by armoured vehicles

Hugh Elles.

the world had ever seen. The Brigadier General's Tank Corps would indeed be 'blooded'.

The Plan for the Cavalry

The Cavalry Corps consisted of four divisions, each with three brigades. The 1st Division was commanded by Major General Mullens, who had led the mad charge of the 4th Dragoons at Audregnies in August 1914; the 2nd by Major General Greenly; the 4th by Major General Kennedy (it had three Indian Army Cavalry Brigades); and the 5th by Major General Macandrew (two Indian and one Canadian brigades), giving a total of approximately 40,000 men. Its task was to pass through the gaps made by the infantry and tanks and then to isolate Cambrai, capture Bourlon Wood and seize the crossings of the Sensée River. All this was to be achieved not later than the night of the 22nd. This would involve a ride of more than ten miles from its forming up position, but the infantry were told they must not wait for the cavalry to arrive before pressing on. The cavalry divisions which were to cross the St Quentin Canal had to move very quickly in order to encircle and cut off Cambrai. One of the special instructions was to prevent the enemy from setting the town on fire; but large bodies of them must not enter the town without infantry and tank support. An early task was to capture the German Army Group's advanced headquarters at Escadoeuvres, in the north-eastern suburbs of Cambrai. All the divisions would have wire pulling tanks waiting for them, but if necessary, efforts should be made to clear the wire on their own initiative. The absolutely vital task was the seizure of the

Cavalry was to play its part once the German line had been broken. In the event it was not to be as planned; but it fought effectively as dismounted infantry.

Sensée crossings. The essence of all the cavalry's action was speed.

The whole Cavalry Corps began its movement forward from its bases about Pèronne at midnight on the 19th/20th, marching to the areas on the southern edge of the bowl, some three miles behind the attack line. Major General Mullens' 1st Division was allotted to IV Corps; it arrived at Fins at 6.15am where a large water tank for the horses had been constructed by the sappers. The division's task included assisting the 6th Division's attack on Premy Chapel, at the eastern end of Flesquières Ridge. Major General Mullens' intention was, if the 51st (Highland) Division made good progress, to launch his leading brigade over the ridge west of Premy Chapel and capture the village of Cantaing, below Fontaine-Notre-Dame.

Shortly before 11.35am two of his brigades, the 1st and 2nd, had arrived at Trescault; whilst at Metz-en-Couture was his 3rd. The other three divisions had arrived at Bonavis Ridge, near Gonnelieu; these would provide the major thrust on Cambrai over the St Quentin Canal. The capture of its bridges intact was vital to their battle plan. There was one other cavalry unit for the attack on Flesquières Ridge: IV Corps' own attached cavalry regiment, King Edward's Horse.

There was one great flaw in the Cavalry Corps' organization. The Cavalry Corps Headquarters remained at Fins, six miles behind the nearest point of the battle front and twelve miles away from the crucial canal bridges. The Corps Commander had specifically given orders to his divisional and brigade commanders that no forward movement must be made without orders from his headquarters. Once the battle began, almost at once most of the telephone lines were destroyed. This caused inevitable and avoidable delays in passing orders down the chain of command from Corps, through division and brigade to regiment. The great opportunity for the cavalry to show how effective it could be was lost.

The Plan for the Infantry

The attack, mainly a north-easterly one heading for Bourlon, was defined in three bounds all heading generally north and curving to the east, ending with a 7,500 yard front from the 'Dry Ditch' on the left to the hill top road junction at Premy Chapel. The first 'bound' an average of 2,500 yards from the British front line (but of 3,000 yards on the left), was colour coded Blue; the second, some 1,500 yards beyond it, Brown; and the last, Red, a further 2,000 yards. This would, on the left, take the Corps almost to the main road from Cambrai to Bapaume. In the centre the Red Line looked towards Bourlon Hill, with Fontaine-Notre-Dame but 3,000 yards from them, and Cantaing 1,000 yards in front. A short distance to the right, in III Corps' sector, was the St Quentin canal.

The most difficult part of the attack was on the left, the 62nd Division's sector. It would attack on a 3,000 yard front with two brigades, the third in support, out of Havrincourt Wood, up the steep slope, with the 'Dry Ditch' on its left. It would get into the Hindenburg Line which surrounded the strongly defended Havrincourt village and its dominating chateau. Once through the village, and onto the Blue line it would be into the main stream of the Hindenburg Line where it ran down from the north, on both sides of the Canal du Nord, its wire and trench lines 1,000 yards deep. Advancing into and through them, the Brown Line was a further 1,500 yards; and from there it would continue for a further 2,000 yards to the strongly defended village of Graincourt, on the British side of the Red line. From here it was a further 1,000 yards to the village of Anneux, the main road and Bourlon Wood.

In the centre, attacking on a 2,550 yard front, was the 51st Division, which would also attack with two brigades. It would go down the slope from Trescault into the Grand Ravine and on to the Blue Line, a few yards west of Ribécourt and 2,500 yards from its jump off point. Then it was up the treeless and steep valley side to the ridge top and Flesquières, the Brown Line curving around its northern edge, an advance of 2,000 yards. Practically from the start it would fight through a 1,000 yard belt of the main Hindenburg Line; but in front of Flesquières and the Brown Line was the Hindenburg Support Line, a less formidable objective. The division would then turn north-easterly

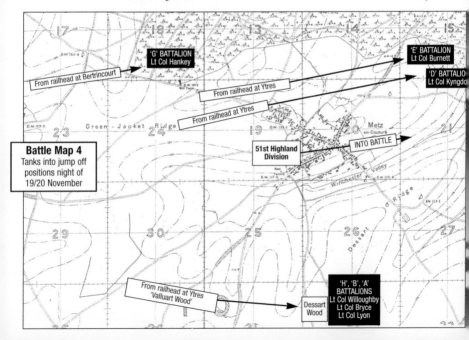

'G' BATTALION Lt Col Hankey

'E' BATTALION Lt Col Burnett

'D' BATTALIO Lt Col Kyngdo

From railhead at Bertrincourt

From railhead at Ytres

From railhead at Ytres

Green - Jacket Ridge

Metz en-Couture

INTO BATTLE

Battle Map 4
Tanks into jump off positions night of 19/20 November

51st Highland Division

From railhead at Ytres 'Valluart Wood'

'H', 'B', 'A' BATTALIONS
Lt Col Willoughby
Lt Col Bryce
Lt Col Lyon

Dessart Wood

to cross the open and flat plain for 1,500 yards to the Red Line; and from there it was 3,000 yards through the long and defended small village of Cantaing to Bourlon Wood, the main road and the gateway to Cambrai at Fontaine-Notre-Dame. Once the Blue and Brown Lines had fallen the two divisions' reserve brigades would take over the advance.

Ribécourt, on the Blue Line, would be attacked by 71 Brigade from the 6th Division. Its 16 and 18 Brigades would then continue up the hill, through the Brown Line, to occupy Premy Chapel and the Red Line about 1,000 yards further east and on to the St Quentin Canal.

The time scale, if all went well, predicted that the advance from the second objective, the Brown Line, would begin 240 minutes from Zero, giving just four hours to advance 5,000 yards through the main depth of the Hindenburg Line: that would be an incredible achievement.

The 51st Division was subsequently to head for Cantaing and the 62nd for Graincourt, Anneux and the western end of Bourlon Wood. The IV Corps' plan was to attack with these two divisions east of the Canal du Nord whilst the 36th (Ulster) Division would advance northwards on the western bank.

A total of sixty tanks would go in front of the 62nd Division and seventy with the 51st. On their right, thirty six would lead 71 Brigade, comprising more than a third of the total tank force available for the battle.

In the early part of November the divisions which would make the attack were withdrawn to the west of Bapaume and Pèronne, the 62nd and 51st from IV Corps and the 6th and 12th from III Corps. In IV Corps' area the 36th Division came into Havrincourt Wood and behind the Trescault Ridge to hold the line there for the 62nd and the 51st. The Ulstermen carried out the additional work imposed upon them very thoroughly, as well as carrying out patrols and minor attacks to give the enemy no inkling of the forthcoming attack. Scrub was gathered and from twigs and bushes a 5,000 yard long screen was hung along the northern edge of the wood, which, surprisingly, was never noticed by the Germans.

Behind it they marked out positions. Ammunition recesses and telephone pits were dug; shelters for the gun detachments and gun platforms were prepared at the pegged out locations; observation posts and brigade headquarters were selected, and huge dumps for ammunition were formed. A large amount of accommodation in the ruined villages was made, and in the woods, shacks for three battalions

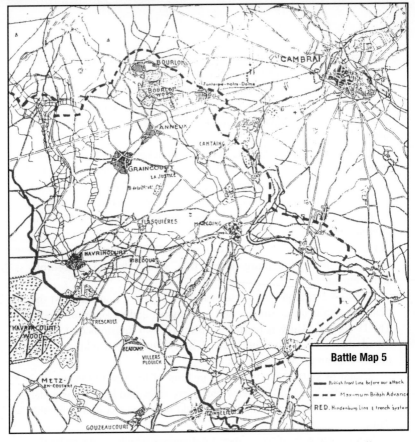

Battle Map 5

British front line before our attack
Maximum British Advance
RED. Hindenburg Line & trench system

were erected, company dugouts prepared, some excavated especially to form battalion headquarters.

The two divisions that would carry out the attack, the 62nd and 51st, used their own engineers on road and communications work, so all of that done by the Ulstermen was with their own manpower. An astonishing amount of work was done, all in the dark.

The 36th Division would also be making an attack up the western side of the Canal Du Nord on the morning of the 20th but only with the one brigade, the 109th. The other two, 107 and 108, after handing over their fronts to the 51st and 62nd Divisions, were kept in Corps Reserve.

In the days before the divisions came into the line parties of officers and NCOs visited it, to make reconnaissances of the particular sector their brigade and battalion would have to attack and capture. When they viewed the battlefield they could see the forbidding, barbed wire filled valley and Flesquières, high on the ridge. They did not know what difficulties the hidden Grand Ravine might hold, but it was thought to be full of water. To maintain secrecy the Highlanders looking at the battlefields wore trousers instead of kilts. For similar reasons, on the night of the 19th, as the West Yorkshire Division began to come into the line, Ulstermen still held the front, and when the few men were captured the enemy simply thought everything was as normal.

All the divisions had their full complement of supporting arms: twelve batteries of artillery; three Field Companies of Royal Engineers, with a Signal Company (and their Pioneers); three Field Ambulances; one Casualty Clearing Station; a Divisional train; four companies of the Army Service Corps and even a Veterinary Section. The ground behind Trescault Ridge teemed with thousands of men and animals

62nd (2nd West Riding) Division
Major General Sir Walter Braithwaite

185 Brigade, *Brigadier General Viscount Hampden*
2/5th, 2/6th, 2/7th, 2/8th, West Yorkshire Regiment

186 Brigade, *Brigadier General Roland B. Bradford VC*
2/4th, 2/5th, 2/6th, 2/7th, Duke of Wellington's Regiment

187 Brigade, *Brigadier General R.O'B. Taylor*
2/4th, 2/5th, York and Lancaster Regiment
2/4th, 2/5th, Kings Own Yorkshire light Infantry

51st (Highland) Division
Major General G.M. Harper

Major General Sir Walter Braithwaite.

152 Brigade, *Brigadier General H.P. Burn*
1/8th Argyll and Sutherland Highlanders
1/5th, 1/6th, Seaforth Highlanders
1/6th Gordon Highlanders

153 Brigade, *Brigadier General A.T. Beckwith*
1/5th, 1/7th, Gordon Highlanders, 1/6th, 1/7th, Black Watch

154 Brigade, *Brigadier General K.G. Buchanan*
1/4th Gordon Highlanders, 1/4th Seaforth Highlanders
1/7th Argyll and Sutherland Highlanders, 1/9th Royal Scots

6th Division's Brigade
71 Brigade, *Brigadier General P.W. Brown*
1/Leicester Regiment, 9/Suffolk Regiment, 9/Norfolk Regiment, 2/Sherwood Foresters

The first attack by the West Yorkshire Division would be made by 185 Brigade on the right, debouching from the north-east part of

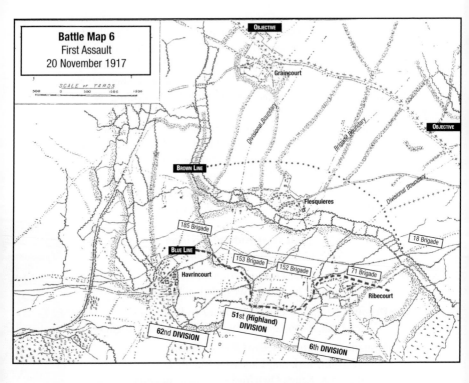

Battle Map 6
First Assault
20 November 1917

SCALE OF YARDS

OBJECTIVE

Graincourt

OBJECTIVE

Divisional Boundary

Brigade Boundary

Divisional Boundary

BROWN LINE

Flesquieres

185 Brigade

18 Brigade

BLUE LINE

153 Brigade

152 Brigade

71 Brigade

Havrincourt

Ribecourt

51st (Highland) DIVISION

62nd DIVISION

6th DIVISION

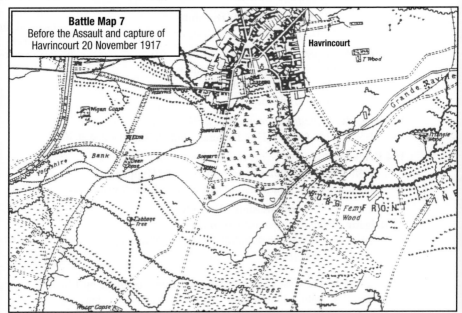

Battle Map 7
Before the Assault and capture of
Havrincourt 20 November 1917

Havrincourt

T Wood

Grande Ravine

Wigan Copse

Snowdon

Yorkshire Bank

Dean Copse

Boggart

Triangle Wood

FRONT LINE

Femy Wood

Cabbage Tree

Water Copse

46

Havrincourt Wood where the trees had been demolished, then through Femy Wood and up the slope, with T Wood in the middle. Its objective was 700 yards east of the village, almost to the second German Line at Chapel Wood. It would take Chapel Trench, running west to east, and take the railway and the Blue Line at the first bound.

187 Brigade, starting out at the same time, would come out of Havrincourt Wood on the left, through the almost treeless Oxford Valley, and take the strong points at Wigan Copse and the fortified mine craters on the central track. It would move up the left hand side of the village, take the huge chateau and proceed to the Blue Line on the northern edge.

It had been planned that 186 Brigade, in reserve, would not advance until the second objective, the Brown Line, had fallen. But Brigadier General Bradford VC, the youngest general in the British Army, was anxious to advance early in the attack and take up a more forward position. This was entirely in his character; still only twenty-five he had won his Victoria Cross just twelve months earlier whilst commanding two battalions of the Durham Light Infantry in the attack on the Butte de Warlencourt in the last battles of 1916 on the Somme. Braithwaite agreed, a decision which was to result in a resounding success for his division. Bradford had only taken the Brigade over a few days earlier, on 10 November.

The night of the 19th was a very anxious time and when, in the morning, just before dawn, the enemy shelled Havrincourt Wood, some thought the Germans had found out about the plan. They had not.

At 3am the battalions ate their breakfast, a hot dixie of tea and sugar, bully beef or tinned fish with bread, and were issued with a good tot of rum. They would advance on a full stomach. A similar performance was going on in the Highland brigades. 153 Brigade would advance on the right of the Yorkshire men, the 51st's left flank and 152 Brigade on the right of the division. The reserve brigade, 154, was billeted at Metz, but would march to the front later that day when the attack was underway. 71 Brigade was waiting in the sunken road between Villers-Plouich and Beaucamp; it would have to fight through 2,000 yards before it could achieve its Blue Line objective at Ribécourt. This village is situated in the bottom of the bowl and at the foot of the Flesquières Ridge.

All that could be done had been done; the Staff had performed an incredible feat of work, issuing orders to cover numerous eventualities and ensuring that whatever would be needed was there to hand. One factor that was overlooked was fatigue (as the Germans were to do in

1918). The infantry were equipped to fight a trench to trench battle carrying at least seventy pounds of kit and equipment. Though a long advance on the first day was planned, hoped for and remarkably achieved – the longest advance the British Army had made in this war – by nightfall most of the men were exhausted. The planners were used to attacks with an advance of just a few hundred yards at best and had forgotten tiredness – or perhaps they had to make best use of the troops available. It was a problem which would have an unfortunate effect in the days to come, particularly when the enemy confronting them was reinforced with fresh troops.

Tuesday 20 November broke dull and misty, with a light wind from the south-west. It was still dark at 6.10am and at 6.30am, under the thunder of a 1,003 gun bombardment and the noise of low flying aircraft, machine guns and bombs, accompanied by the engine noise of the moving tanks, the infantry went forward. They could see the enemy's lines lit up by flame, their SOS rockets bursting in the darkness of the morning. The Battle of Cambrai had begun.

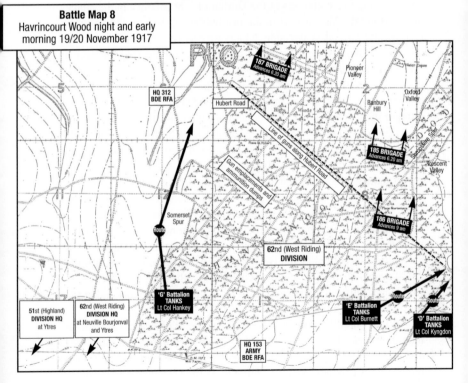

Battle Map 8
Havrincourt Wood night and early morning 19/20 November 1917

Chapter Two

THE ATTACK ON FLESQUIÈRES RIDGE

The 62nd (2nd West Riding) Division: The Left Flank.

At 6.20am Major General Sir Walter Braithwaite's men began their attack with 185 Brigade on the right and 187 Brigade on the left. Its left flank battalion, the 2/5th KOYLIs, was between the Canal du Nord and the track running north from Dean Copse to the Havrincourt to Hermies track. The right hand battalion of 185 Brigade and of the division was the 2/7th West Yorks, whose first objective was Triangle Wood. This gave a divisional front of 3,000 yards. Facing it was the strongest part of the Hindenburg Line, more than 1,000 yards wide.

To lead the Division there would be more than sixty tanks, the whole of G Battalion supplemented with sixteen tanks from D and E. In front would go four of them specifically to crush and cut the wire. Unfortunately only fifty tanks had arrived due to mechanical breakdowns and the deadly hazards of tree stumps, fallen trees and deep trenches. Nevertheless the 2/7th West Yorks could not wait and advanced without any tank support as the enemy's artillery began to shell the valley in front of Trescault, through which they were advancing. C Company, whose job it was to capture the outpost line so that the 2/8th West Yorks (Leeds Rifles) could pass through to the first objective, pressed forward, quickly overcoming the enemy, taking a 100 prisoners and four machine guns. The importance of mopping up captured positions had been impressed on everybody. Too often in the past places had been taken only to be quickly lost again because the resourceful Germans had hidden in dugouts to come out attacking the infantry in the rear. C Company quickly consolidated the area; then the tanks arrived and four companies of the 2/8th came through.

Thirty minutes after setting off the battalion had reached the main Hindenburg Line. The tanks had done their work very well, the Germans completely shattered by the ferocious bombardment and the fearsome tanks. Female tanks had cruised up and down the German trench lines, machine gunning the terrorised men of Captain Soltau's 84th Regiment, and were soon followed by the enthusiastic infantry. This was too much for the Germans, who soon capitulated. Some had resisted, and these were shot or bayoneted out of the holes where they were hiding. Another eighty men surrendered, along with six more machine guns.

Battle Map 9
62nd West Yorkshire Division

Brigadier R. B. Bradford killed here
Lock 7

BROW LINE

14   15   16

Dry canal 62nd Division boundary

62nd Division boundary

Height in feet from ground level to canal bottom

Spoil Heap

20   21   22   BLUE LINE

Chapel

Chapel Wood

186 BRIGADE

Havrincourt   T Wood

Canal Copse   Station   28

Gorge Bridge   Church

26   Lt Col Best killed   Chateau & Wood

Vesuvius

187 BRIGADE   Wigan Copse

Etna   Snowden   185 BRIGADE   Triangle Wood

Boggart Hole

32   33   Femy Wood

Dean Copse

50

A Company of the West Yorks stayed to mop up but three companies, now with the tanks, advanced to the next objective, Triangle Wood, a small copse immediately behind the main line, fortified with infantry and machine guns. The West Yorks were expecting to see the Gordon Highlanders from 153 Brigade, but they had not arrived. They could not wait, speed having been impressed upon them from the start, so the wood was attacked from both sides and quickly fell. Twenty-nine prisoners and another machine gun were taken. The Yorkshiremen had not taken the position without losses; B Company on the right, supporting the attack, was hit by long range machine gun fire from Ribécourt and lost forty men. D Company on the left, now heading past the wood, lost all its officers and a senior sergeant took command. The battalion now crossed the western end of the feared Grand Ravine, which turned out not to be the obstacle they had anticipated. They climbed the valley slope up to the eastern side of Havrincourt in the face of machine gun fire coming down from a small T shaped copse 600 yards ahead. The men bombed and bayoneted two of the crew, the rest scattered, running for their lives. However, the 2/8th were then held up by machine gun fire coming from a concrete bunker further up the hill. Continuing to advance, they killed twenty more Germans and took sixty-three prisoners, including three officers.

It now was three hours after the attack had started but the battalion still had another task to do. Assisted by some tanks it attacked Chapel Trench, which connected Chapel Wood on the right to Havrincourt, near the railway line. By 10am it had fallen, many Germans were killed and 110 prisoners taken.

On orders being received from Brigade HQ, situated in the top right hand corner of Havrincourt Wood, the battalion mopped up and consolidated in Chapel Trench and by 1 pm formed a defensive front on the railway embankment 400 yards to the north-east; it had reached the Blue Line.

The 2/6th West Yorks, on the left of 185 Brigade, had been struggling against determined opposition; they and the 2/5th had run into Captain Soltau and his defenders at their best. At the start six tanks were detailed to lead the 2/5th to make an opening for the 2/6th, however two of the tanks never arrived. For over an hour the 2/5th battled to break into the Outpost Line but could not advance on the right of the 2/6th, which eventually succeeded in breaking in. However, C Company had many casualties. Its A Company had pushed forward without the support of any tanks through the Hindenburg Main Line and had established a strong line on the track coming out of the Grand

Havrincourt Chateau.

Ravine to the south-eastern corner of Havrincourt village leading straight into the chateau grounds. The battalion was swept with machine gun fire from the chateau and the houses in the village but with the support of a tank (a Male, G3) part of the battalion entered the village. Six tanks had been knocked out before this one arrived.

Making its way to the main street under heavy machine gun fire from the men of the 84th Regiment, the tank encountered a large water filled shell crater or mine hole. It caught fire and the crew, struggling to get out, were hit by bullets, two being killed instantly. Five others, all wounded, got into a small shell hole. About 100 of the enemy now came out of their hiding places and advanced with a rush to the tank. The tank commander, Second Lieutenant McElroy, was still inside and heroically held them off with his revolver, killing eight of them. The attack stopped, he put out the fire and kept the enemy at bay with one of the Lewis guns for almost an hour until rescued by British infantry when the Germans surrendered. He was awarded the DSO.

Whilst this personal battle was taking place in the village the chateau was still occupied by determined Germans; yet part of 185 Brigade were on the Blue Line. Lieutenant Colonel Hoare's 2/6th had suffered badly. By 10.15am it had lost seven officers and 150 other ranks.

On the left flank of 187 Brigade, 2/4th KOYLIs on the right and 2/5th KOYLIs on the left set off late. At Zero + 15, when the tanks scheduled to lead the 2/4th had not arrived, following Brigadier General Taylor's instruction that tanks or no tanks the attack must start on time, at 6.35am the men went forward as the barrage fell on the German trenches. Fortunately the tanks caught up, smashing down the barbed wire. One broke down almost immediately but the

Brigadier General Hampden, commanding 185 Brigade.

rest carried on. The infantry broke into the Outpost Line and the enemy in the small garrisons there, appalled at the sudden violent shelling and at the sight of the steel monsters coming towards them, had no stomach for a fight and quickly surrendered. The battalion's right flank was against Oxford Road, on the right of Oxford Valley. Machine gun fire swept into the Yorkshire men from two directions, both about 500 yards away. One came from near a large pond, fed in winter time by small streams running into the Grand Ravine, and the other from Havrincourt Park. The battalion's next obstacle was the fortified Boggart Hole and then, 300 yards further along the track, a fortified mine crater, Snowden. The tanks fell on both of these and the garrisons were soon eliminated by bomb and bayonet.

Five hundred yards to the left of the battalion there was a track running up from Dean Copse. Blown into the track was another crater Etna, which was also fortified. This was the 2/5th's right flank objective but the tank allotted for the task had not arrived; therefore the 2/4th, whose objectives had fallen fairly easily, sent a platoon to help and with two of the 2/5th's – about a 100 men in all – attacked the stronghold. Working forward through the ruins of Dean Copse, Etna was rushed and another machine gun and seventeen prisoners were added to the fast growing list of captures.

On the right, the 2/4th was still being attacked by a number of machine guns firing from the wood behind Havrincourt chateau manned by some of the redoubtable Captain Soltau's men. Some of these brave men continued to fight from the chateau's cellars and upper rooms even when the rest of the village had fallen into British hands. Some of the KOYLIs got into the wood and, after a hard fight, seventy prisoners with two machine guns were taken.

Both battalions were now getting closer to the road from Havrincourt to the blown bridge over the 100 feet deep cutting at the Canal du Nord, at a point where the 500 yard long track from Dean Copse joins the east to west one from Havrincourt. Here was a further deep mine crater, Vesuvius, with a strong garrison whose machine guns were firing down the steep valley side onto the attackers.

A joint effort by platoons from both battalions made a pincer movement and once again the enemy, fighting until the last moment, were eliminated. Two machine guns and fourteen men were captured, leaving many dead, most killed by the bayonet. Over on the left, close to the Canal, was a small square copse named by the 42nd (East Lancs) Division Wigan Copse. The 2/5th quickly overran the demoralised defenders and, crossing the east to west track near the demolished bridge, arrived at a strongly held trench in a sunken road. Here Captain Lynn with Second Lieutenant James and their men set about the enemy there who had seen the British progress and were determined to stop it. The trench was occupied with speed and it became a hand-to-hand battle, the Captain personally killed four whilst James accounted for no fewer than eighteen with bombs, bullets and bayonet. None of the enemy escaped, it was a fight to the finish, all of them being either killed or wounded. Both of these valiant officers had actually gone out the previous night, anticipating that the tanks might not arrive and had cut the wire, reconnoitring the route they would take and laying out white tapes to guide them.

The remaining companies of the battalion could now advance and at about 8.15am it had reached the Blue Line, a 1,000 yards west of the village and almost 2,000 yards from the beginning of its advance. It had captured more than 400 prisoners, eight machine guns and four trench mortars.

The fighting had not yet ceased in the village. The 2/4th were in among the houses, which still held many of the German 84th Regiment with machine guns and snipers. These fired down onto the attackers.

One of them, a brave man, had mounted a machine gun at the village square but he was soon killed. At about 8.30am the Blue Line had been reached all along the division's front but it would take a further two hours before the chateau was finally cleared of the few remaining defenders.

The KOYLIs in their advance had by no means been unscathed: the 2/4th suffered five officers killed and six wounded out of twenty committed and 211 other ranks casualties. The 2/5th suffered somewhat less: three officers wounded and 120 other ranks casualties. Captain Soltau had at last withdrawn out of the village, still hoping to delay the enemy's advance with a stand in a farmhouse. He and the few men still with him were all killed shortly afterward.

At 7am the two rear battalions of each of the attacking brigades, the 2/4th and 2/5th York and Lancs, and the 2/5th and 2/7th West Yorks, were ready to move. They were to start off from the Blue Line at 8.35am.

The 2/5th York and Lancs were to advance on the western side of the village, go slowly round its north-west side and then, changing direction, go north of it to the Brown Line. They encountered some machine gun fire from Havrincourt and took casualties. The 2/4th York and Lancs (Hallamshires), coming up on the far left, with the left hand man looking down into the canal, were untroubled, apart from the odd desperately brave man and the huge tangle of barbed wire, and arrived on time. Havrincourt village was still not yet empty of the enemy. Two battalions of the West Yorks, the 2/5th and the 2/7th, would deal with

Canal Du Nord in 62nd Yorkshire (West Riding) Division's sector.

those men and then move through the village to the Blue Line, ready to advance at 10am on the Brown Line.

Thus, the rim at the western end of Flesquières Ridge had been taken, albeit with a considerable loss of men and tanks. Forty of the latter would get to the Brown Line but something like thirty had been stopped by either the difficult terrain or mechanical breakdowns and twelve by enemy action; dozens of the men in them were wounded or killed.

On the eastern side of the Canal du Nord, 109 Brigade of the 36th (Ulster) Division started its attack northwards at 8.35am, just when the 2/5th KOYLIs had just reached the canal bank opposite the arrow head shaped fortified spoil heap on the western side. The 10th Royal Inniskilling Fusiliers, supported by a heavy artillery barrage, stormed the fortress; the Germans, shaken by the battle going on behind them, made little resistance, many surrendering or fleeing northward. The Inniskillings then continued to push along the wide barbed wire barricades and deep trenches on the western side, making the eventual advance of the 62nd Division on that flank much easier.

The Ulstermen, reinforced by more battalions of the brigade, continued their advance, reaching the track from Graincourt to Demicourt above Lock 7 and 2,500 yards north of the Spoil Heap. There had been no tanks with them.

Whilst the battle for Havrincourt had been taking place the four battalions of the Duke of Wellington's Regiment, many of them

German trenches in Bois d' Havrincourt.

Halifax men, who has spent a comfortable night in billets four miles to the west in Bertincourt, had an early hot breakfast and then at 5.20am set off for their assembly positions in Havrincourt Wood.

At 8am 186 Brigade, with six tanks from 'G' Battalion, was in position facing north-east about the crossroads on the eastern side of the wood, at Hubert Road and the Shropshire Spur. Over to the right they could see Trescault and the battle for Flesquières taking place. The 2/6th and 2/4th Battalions with 186 Trench Mortar Battery were on the right, south-east of Shropshire Spur Road; the 2/5th and 2/7th were on the north-western side of it. Already the Brigade's Machine Gun Company (the 213th) was in action in the top north-eastern corner of the wood, at Butlers Cross, supporting the existing attack. At 9am, eager to get into the fray, Brigadier General Bradford moved his men forward, warning them that pockets of the enemy might still exist and must be eradicated as they went.

The division had only been in France since January 1917 but had already suffered 4,000 casualties; the Dukes had new men and for many this was to be their first time in a major battle. They would see some terrible sights as they picked their way through the mass of tumbled barbed wire, the ground strewn with casualties of war from both sides. Men from their own West Riding Field Ambulances were dealing with the wounded, British and German, whilst some of the dead were hastily buried on the spot to be collected and reinterred later.

Three battalions (in the order 2/6th, 2/4th and 2/7th) advanced in companies in columns of fours, deploying once out of the shelter of Shropshire Spur into artillery formation. Their route north-eastwards lay round the bottom of Havrincourt village, through Femy Wood and north towards T Wood. The 2/5th marched along Oxford Road and passed Boggart Hole and Snowden before going to the west of the village.

Three squadrons of the 1st King Edward's Horse also moved into Havrincourt Wood, along with tanks their special task was to seize some bridges on the main road and attack Graincourt.

Going round the eastern side of Havrincourt, the 2/6th came under shell fire from Flesquières; at this time, about 10am, Major General Harper's Highlanders had not yet taken that village. Despite this the battalion continued to advance to the Blue Line, followed by the 2/4th in support and the 2/7th on the right.

They were moving on the Brown Line and at 11am commenced their attack against some very strong trenches known as Hughes Switch and Hughes Support. These trenches were 700 yards long with a 400 yard barbed wire thick gap between them; they connected the north to south stretch of the Hindenburg Support Line with the Canal Du Nord.

The other two Brigades, 185 and 187, remained slightly north of the Brown Line, acting in support of the Dukes. The 2/5th had run into trouble in Havrincourt. At 9.15am they were marching in column towards the left (west) of the village, which they thought had been cleared; on approaching Chateau Wood, part of the chateau's grounds, they were hit by heavy machine gun and rifle fire from the wood and chateau buildings and almost at once Lieutenant Colonel TD Best DSO was killed, as was Lieutenant Bodker. Two other officers, Lieutenants JA Haigh and WL Thomas, were badly wounded; twenty six other ranks were also casualties. The Adjutant, Captain H Jackson handed over command to Captain F Sykes; whilst most of the battalion kept moving forward, Captain T Goodall with his men from D Company, infuriated at the loss of their colonel, attacked the enemy there. They took prisoner one officer and fifty eight other ranks, smashing two machine guns. They also found in the chateau two British PoWs: an officer from IV Corps Headquarters who had been captured whilst on an intelligence gathering mission, and a sergeant of the KOYLIs.

Major General Braithwaite was now concerned that Flesquières had not fallen. At 1pm he suggested to Major General Harper that his Yorkshiremen might make a flanking attack on Flesquières but no action was taken. Therefore he issued an order at 1.35pm forbidding any movement beyond Graincourt or north of the Cambrai-Bapaume road and directed that all available tanks should be rallied and sent against Flesquières from the west. Orders were difficult to transmit over the long distance of the battlefield and with the considerable communications problems which were a feature of the war. Brigadier General Bradford, ignorant of these proceedings, continued to attack.

Although not really involved in the battle for Flesquières Ridge, the Ulstermen of 109 Brigade, 36th Division, had bombed their way along the Hindenburg Line's trenches on the Canal du Nord's west bank. By midday they were being enfiladed from the Hughes Trenches, not yet captured by the Dukes. The Ulstermen had run out of bombs, so a halt was called until 2pm, by when supplies should have arrived and it was hoped that Brigadier General Bradford's men would have taken both Hughes defence lines. They were able to proceed and by dusk the 36th Division had arrived at and beyond the main road and had taken 500 prisoners from the 384th Landwehr Regiment, a second line unit.

Meanwhile the 2/5th Dukes moved into the deepest part of the

Hindenburg Line, a 'U' shaped system of trenches and barbed wire. The advance to the Hughes Switch Line was met with heavy machine gun and rifle fire, the enemy somewhat recovered from their shock of the morning. They had seen many tanks knocked out and set on fire, so that their fear of them considerably lessened. Lieutenant Black was sent forward with his platoon to deal with this defensive firing, but soon ran into a battle in full progress. He found a ditched tank deep in the Support Line close to the strong point for which he was heading. The tank commander and his crew were outside the machine and defending it with their Lewis guns. Lieutenant Black continued and managed to work around the strong point, rushing it and killing those that resisted. He took five prisoners, but the rest of the surviving garrison fled towards Graincourt only to be cut down by British Lewis guns.

The 2/5th Battalion reorganized. They had suffered a large number of casualties in their 3,000 yard advance, whilst ahead was the next objective, Kangaroo Alley, 1,000 yards away, to the west of Graincourt. It was a deep trench line connecting the track from Graincourt to Moeuvres with the Canal du Nord at Lock 6. The canal at this stage was partially completed, dug with some concreted parts, but contained no water.

With D Company still leading, and B Company on the right, both accompanied by a number of tanks, Kangaroo Alley and Lock 6 (captured by C Company) were soon taken after a short but stiff battle. One hundred and sixteen prisoners were taken, including four officers, and more machine guns. At the lock a number of Germans refused to come out so a bomb was hurled into their dugout, destroying it and the occupants.

By dusk the day was over for the 2/5th, they were only 500 yards from the main Cambrai – Bapaume road and had captured more than 350 prisoners and fifteen machine guns. In addition to losing their colonel and Lieutenant Bodker, Lieutenant J. Haigh also died from the wounds he received in Havrincourt, Lieutenant W. Thomas was wounded and 69 other ranks were killed or wounded.

At midday two squadrons of King Edward's Horse had moved out of the wood with the intention of moving on Graincourt and Anneux, the latter a small, strung out village 3,000 yards north of Flesquières, 1,000 yards east of Graincourt and just 400 yards from the main road and the south-west corner of Bourlon Wood. However the cavalry could do nothing until Graincourt had fallen, which it had not, and the horsemen had to await their opportunity. Later in the day they were to

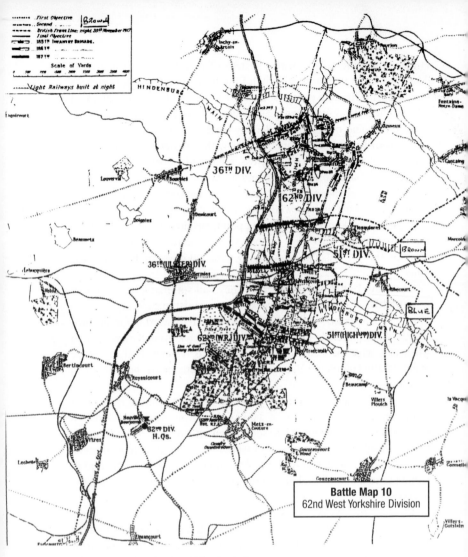

Battle Map 10
62nd West Yorkshire Division

fight dismounted alongside the infantry.

The 2/4th, 2/6th and 2/7th Dukes had continued their attack towards Graincourt, behind and slightly to the right of the 2/5th. Graincourt was now cut off from any help from the north-west, and Bradford was determined to take both it and Anneux that day. He considered that this would provide a good start line for the attack on Bourlon on the following morning. At this stage he was unaware of the failure at Flesquières. He moved forward in the early afternoon and ordered the 2/4th to attack Graincourt with the 2/6th close behind on the right and the 2/7th in support. All the tanks that could be gathered were to support the attack. Once the assault started, with tanks leading, it was soon discovered that some 77mm field guns, operating in an anti-tank role, were dug in before the village. With surprising speed six tanks were knocked out, but three Male tanks then arrived and destroyed some of the guns with their six pounders, the crews of the remainder fleeing into the houses. The leading company of the 2/4th arrived at the village and halted to await the arrival of the rest of the battalion. On getting there the two left companies, C and D, led by a Male tank, entered the village under stiff opposition from riflemen and machine guns in the buildings. The 2/6th slid sideways, advancing on Anneux whilst the 2/7th was in support of both and two squadrons of the Corps Cavalry Regiment, King Edward's Horse, left their horses behind and came up as infantrymen; the cavalry were armed with the standard infantry rifle. The 2/7th moved north to the 2/6th, but were held up by a strong force and also halted. They were urged on by their aggressive Brigadier General and passed through towards the main road.

The 2/4th overcame Graincourt at about 3.30pm and established a line north of the village, taking the large buildings of the Sugar Factory at the road. Brigadier General Bradford was in the village only minutes after it had fallen and without delay sent a small patrol of tanks to see what lay ahead on the road to Bourlon. On their return he was told that the enemy was in full retreat and that the village was free to be taken. However by now he had received the news that the divisional commander had ordered no further advances to be made that day. Bradford obeyed.

The 2/6th had now removed the obstruction, mainly with bombs and bayonet, and along with the dismounted cavalry continued in the dusk to Anneux. The village was packed with Germans. All the battalions were withdrawn into Graincourt by about 10pm except for one company of the 2/4th, which stayed in the Sugar Factory until orders for the morrow were received. Bradford put his HQ in the ancient catacombs beneath the large, badly damaged church which a heavy artillery group had bombarded for four hours during the morning.

B Company under Lieutenant Knowles had captured the Sugar Factory in the late afternoon, and as dusk fell set about establishing posts around the building. Second Lieutenant Castle rushed to place some men along the main road. As it was almost dark he was in a hurry. Accompanied by his platoon sergeant, Sergeant Kingham, they were looking for a good position when they saw a body of men with fixed bayonets in column of route approaching about twenty yards away and marching towards Cambrai. It was too dark to see the head of the column, but there seemed to be more than a 100 men. His own men were too far away to take advantage of this and he could not attempt to capture them all. So, very silently, he and the sergeant rushed to cut off the last rank of three. With his revolver against the centre man's nose and levelling his left hand as though it was a pistol at another. Kingham covered the third man with his bayonet. The three Germans tried to get their rifles free, but Castle hit the centre man hard on the nose with his pistol. They stopped and put up their hands, surprisingly without a murmur, whilst the remainder of the Germans, blissfully unaware, simply carried on marching.

Castle dashed back to his platoon with his captives. Meeting Private Bradbury with his Lewis gun and some others, Castle ordered them to fire down the road. It was pitch dark but they were bound to hit someone and at least it would send the Germans on their way very quickly. The three prisoners turned out to be an officer, who spoke excellent English, a corporal and a private. Castle learnt that the column was 200 strong and had just passed through Cambrai that afternoon to reinforce their line. Ignorant of the area they had turned around to seek shelter in Bourlon Wood for the night. Castle then hurried his prisoners back to the factory and told his commander of the action, suggesting that as the Germans were obviously quite close sections should be posted to watch for them. In fact during the night a number of small scale attempts were made on the factory; Lieutenant Knowles' men held them off. Later it was estimated, when bodies were found along the road, that as many as fifty had been killed from the column by Second Lieutenant Castle's men.

At the end of the day Major General Braithwaite had his 186 Brigade grouped in and around Graincourt, ready for the advance against Bourlon. He was delighted that Bradford's gamble had paid off. He would deal with the strongly held little village of Anneux at dawn.

Meanwhile the tank men were struggling to replenish what machines they had left. Almost all of them were too low on fuel to go much further and the crews had to recover from the ghastly conditions that they had endured. Many of them were wounded or sick and had to be replaced with the few others who came up from Havrincourt Wood.

During the morning, as the battle had progressed north, the 461 Field Company Royal Engineers, who had come into the wood at 9am, began a hard day's essential work, undeterred by desultory shelling and sniping from enemy who had not yet been cleared. They started to clear the barricades of trees, brush, sandbags and the masses of barbed wire littering the badly damaged tracks. It started to rain, as it would all day, turning the tracks everywhere into deep mud. Craters had to be filled in with whatever material was to hand. Deviations were created by sleepers and tree trunks round the deeper mine holes, particularly Etna and Vesuvius, which were preventing motor ambulances from using this one decent road. By 11am their work had improved the road a distance of 3,250 yards sufficiently enough to permit movement of the first line transport, machine gun vehicles, wheeled ambulances, and ammunition and trench mortar carts. The many wounded had to be

German prisoners being used as stretcher bearers and to assist at a dressing station.

removed as quickly as possible. As always stretcher bearers were few in number as many had been knocked out in the advance.

At midday a battery of artillery, B/310, galloped forward to the north east of the wood in support of 185 Brigade. It was said "to be a 'most inspiring sight to see six horse teams trotting along, pulling 18 Pounders over the grassy open fields below Graincourt as though they were at Larkhill on Salisbury Plain".
As they went they came across eight 77mm field guns with limbers full of ammunition, similar to their own; the gunners used them against the previous owners, saving their own guns for the future.

Later in the evening, in preparation for Bradford's attack on Bourlon the following morning, twenty more tanks were scraped together from the Corps Reserve, and the 11th Hussars (Prince Albert's Own) from the 1st Cavalry Brigade came into the wood en route to Bradford's Brigade.

By noon on the first day Major General Braithwaite had two brigades with almost nothing to do. Since capturing the Brown Line they had dug in, using captured German trenches of the Hindenburg Support and facing north-eastwards. From these they could watch 186 Brigade's attack towards Graincourt. One can only speculate as to what might have happened if his troops had attacked the flank of Flesquières, or if his troops had pressed on to the main road to the north. This would have left them prepared for an early morning assault on Bourlon and the possibilities for a cavalry advance that success there would have provided. But a division action on its own could be dangerously exposed on its flanks and would outrun its artillery support. Braithwaite had no real alternative but to do as he did. He was proud of his men's achievements: they had advanced 7,000 yards on this first day, no other British advance of the war so far had got further; they had taken 2,000 prisoners and many items of equipment – artillery, including one complete battery of 5.9's, machine guns and trench mortars – but not without a high cost in British casualties. There were 79 officers and 1,569 other ranks, killed, wounded or missing. During the next three days that figure would be doubled.

The Tank Corps had also suffered badly in that long advance. Some sixty-five tanks had been committed and thirty-four were put out of action, seventeen by mechanical failure and seventeen by enemy action; only nineteen rallied at dusk. Of the crews, 124 were casualties: fifteen killed and the remainder wounded.

There would be one other tragedy, though not associated with their taking of the western end of Flesquières Ridge. Ten days later the

Division was resting in the villages of Bertincourt, Beaumetz and Lebucquière, about five miles west of the Canal du Nord. On 30 November, 186 Brigade was ordered forward in a hurry. Bradford went ahead, placing his HQ in the dry and empty excavations of Lock 7, 2,000 yards south-west of Graincourt. German shelling had already started, the prelude to their counter-attack, when one of the projectiles hit his HQ, mortally wounding him. Braithwaite wrote of him,

He was a very exceptional man. Though only a boy, he might have risen, in fact would have risen, to any height in his profession. He certainly knew every officer in his Brigade although he had only commanded it for a short time and I honestly believe he knew every non commissioned officer and a great many of the privates. He had an extraordinary personality and that, linked with his undoubted military genius, made him a very extraordinary character and a valuable commander of men. His services during the battle can hardly be too highly praised.

Lieutenant Colonel HE Nash, commanding 2/4th Duke of Wellington's Regiment, took over the command of the Brigade.

The 6th Division (III Corps): The Right Flank

6th Division was the left flanking division of III Corps. It was a Regular Army division which had arrived in France during September 1914 and fought in the battle of the Aisne. Originally its brigades were 16, 17, and 18. However, in early 1916, before the Battle of the Somme, some of the New Army Divisions were 'stiffened' by experienced formations and it lost 17 Brigade to the 24th Division, receiving in exchange the 71st, which then consisted of the 1st Leicestershire Regiment, 9th Norfolk Regiment, 9th Suffolk Regiment and 2nd Sherwood Foresters. It was this brigade which would take part, on the left flank of the division and on the right of the Highlanders, in the attack on Flesquières Ridge. 16 Brigade would go forward with it on the right whilst 18 Brigade would be in reserve; it was to follow through and take the Brown Line when Ribécourt had fallen. Brigadier General PW Brown commanded 71 Brigade. The 6th Division was encamped in the Péronne area and would have a long approach march to get into position before 6am on 'Z' Day.

The task of the division was to sweep north-easterly as far as Noyelles on the left bank of the River Escaut which ran parallel to, and a few yards west of, the St. Quentin Canal; it would protect the left flank of the 29th Division coming up on the right once it had taken the bridges lower down over the St Quentin Canal. It would cover the 51st

German soldiers in the village of Anneux prior to the battle.

(Highland) Division's right flank after it had captured Flesquières and then turn easterly, heading for Cantaing and Fontaine-Notre-Dame. Major General Marden had a difficult job, as much depended on these two flanking divisions achieving their objectives.

The divisional artillery had been reinforced by extra batteries. It would, initially, be better protected from close German observation than those guns belonging to the divisions before Havrincourt. However the land was open and fairly devoid of trees south of the Trescault and Bonavis Ridges, and therefore the problem was one of careful advance and camouflage. He would also have difficulty in getting them forward over the open ground once the enemy had recovered from the initial shock. If all did not go according to plan then he could be in trouble from a counter bombardment from the east side of the St Quentin Canal.

The division's supporting tanks had a more difficult approach and their hiding places were far to the south, perhaps 7,000 yards from their jumping off point. They were laid up in Dessart Wood, two miles to the south of Metz-en-Couture, in Heudecourt, two miles south of Gouzeaucourt and in Gauche Wood, between Villers Guislain and Gouzeaucourt. It would be a slow, very quiet drive in the dark of the night of the 19th, following white tapes. H and B Battalions would lead the division; seventy two tanks would, it was hoped, lead the assault.

71 Brigade would capture the village of Ribécourt, in the valley at the foot of the ridge. The attack would be in three waves with the support of a total of thirty six tanks from H Battalion. 16 Brigade, with thirty six tanks from B Battalion would attack at the same time on the right, heading for Marcoing and Noyelles. 18 Brigade, without tanks, would follow up four hours later, move through the eastern end of Ribécourt and advance on Premy Chapel and Nine Wood to form a right flank guard for the 51st (Highland) Division's attack on Cantaing and Fontaine-Notre-Dame and supporting 16 Brigade at Noyelles.

Between 15 – 17 November the 6th Division, along with the 12th and 29th from III Corps and the 51st from IV Corps reached Péronne from their training areas. On the 17th and 18th the 6th Division advanced to the British Front Line to take over its position for the attack on the 20th, The positions and previously been held by the 20th Division, which itself was due to attack at the same time and day.

On arrival the brigades put out observation posts to look at their objectives. From the ruins of the Beet Factory on the north side of Beaucamp and in the centre of 71 Brigade's position on Argyll Ridge, its observing officer could look down at Ribécourt, 3,000 yards below. He could also see the eastern end of the Grand Ravine and from there across the 2,000 yards width of the Brigade's front. He could only see the tops of buildings there, but beyond it the valley side rose steeply to Flesquières Ridge and in the distance he could see the flat land and two or three miles further the great bulk of Bourlon Wood. To the right, the spires of Cambrai were visible. Closer to his position, and perhaps of more immediate interest to him, there were to his right front, the western side of Highland Ridge and on the side of the valley, just to his left, a large group of trees, known as Boar Copse. Five hundred yards in front of the British trench line (here named Beaucamp and Village Support) was the start of the barbed wire and front edge of the Hindenburg Line. The wire seemed to go on for ever but he could not see it all due to the undulating ground; in fact there was a depth of a

Captured German 77mm gun and the tank 'Gorgonzola' at Graincourt on Flesquières ridge.

187 Brigade attack the position known as the 'Spoil Heap'.

1,000 yards of barbed wire barrier and deep trenches. On his map he could pick out Plush Trench (the name an easy corruption of Plouich from the nearby village), the enemy Outpost Line and Beaucamp Switch, in the front line. He could not however, actually see these trenches which were the first objectives. He could follow Argyll Road going down to Ribécourt, the centre line for the brigade's attack. Again he could not see the main, double line of trenches at the front of the Hindenburg Line, Unseen Support, Valley Support, Unseen Trench and Valley Trench. To his left, running down from the ridge and taking in the western edge of Boar Copse, was 71 Brigade's left flank at Lancaster Road. There were no signs of any Germans but he knew that they were there, odd wisps of smoke coming up from the cooking fires. In the very early morning of Monday the 19th he began to see activity behind him as the artillery started to come into its well hidden allotted positions. During that night the observer would have heard the infantry battalions coming forward into the trenches and make out the sound of tank engines.

71 Brigade's attack would be in three stages, each supported by tanks. The first stage would be made by the 1/Leicesters on the left and 9/Suffolk on the right. Their task was to break into the Hindenburg Line through Plush Trench and on for a further 800 yards to the double line of barbed wire and trenches, Unseen Trench.

The second stage would come thirty minutes later, led by half of the Sherwood Foresters (C and D Companies) and 9/Norfolks, taking the double line along with Mole Trench, 400 yards beyond Ribécourt. The Blue Line here ran across the railway line from the station, 500 yards north of the village's ruined church, and then went south-easterly around the village and down towards Couillet Valley. The third stage

Battle Map 11
62nd West Yorkshire Division
captures the ridge

69

would be made by the other half of the Sherwood Foresters: A Company led by Second Lieutenant Fielding (the commander, Captain Shaw MC had been on leave and could not get forward to take his men over the top), and B Company, led by Captain Brown, who had recently been commissioned from sergeant and who had received his promotion just before the battle. They would be joined by the 11/Essex from 18 Brigade. The Essex would first clear the village and then, with the rest of the brigade, head for the double trenched Hindenburg Line, the Brown Line, 1,000 yards beyond the eastern end of Flesquières Ridge. Together with 16 Brigade on their right they would head for the Red Line on Premy Chapel Ridge.

Before the battle the 9/Suffolks' commander, Lieutenant Colonel F Latham DSO, a substantive captain in the 1/Leicesters and now holding temporary rank, had his battalion billeted in a tented camp in Dessart Wood. On the night of the 19/20th he brought them out, following the tanks of H Battalion along the white tapes, to lie down in the open behind the first wave. He would follow six tanks, 100 yards behind as they set off at 6.10am. They would move through the Sherwood Foresters at 6.20am and into No Man's Land to the right of the 1/Leicesters, heading for the German front line at Plush Trench.

In the crucial days before the attack the activities of 9/Norfolks gives an idea of what the battalions preparing for the attack were doing. The Norfolks practised tactics with the tanks at Lignereuil, five miles west of Arras. A model of Ribécourt was made with tape and piles of sawdust and deep trenches were dug to simulate those with which the battalion would have to deal.

The Norfolks lived comparatively well in Lignereuil; they had a wooden hutted camp and a good canteen in which the division's concert party, 'The Fancies', performed. They held rifle and Lewis gun competitions and practised following the tanks in file and wire cutting in case the tanks failed to turn up. On 11 November, the CO with two company commanders (A and C) went on a reconnaissance to look at their battlefield. Lignereuil a practice attack was made on the reproduced trenches, controlled by Lieutenant Dye who would be mortally wounded in front of Ribécourt on the 20th. On the 14th, ten per cent of the battalion were taken out of the attack, which included men on leave. This 10% (and often more) was standard practice, leaving a cadre on which to reform the Battalion should the casualties be heavy.

On the 15th the Norfolks left the training area and marched towards the battle area, moving to Manancourt, two miles west of Fins, where the cavalry were gathering. They had been appalled to see the total destruction of the villages they had passed through, 'A standing monument to the military thoroughness of the enemy', according to the Battalion's war diarist. On the following night they went forward to Dessart Wood and into a wooden hutted camp, already crowded with tank and other battalions and supporting units. It provided the opportunity for the infantry officers to discuss the battle with the officers of their supporting tank H Battalion.

On the 17th the 9/Norfolks went forward into the sunken road at Beaucamp and relieved the 10/Rifle Brigade of the 20th Division, who had been holding the line. The latter would also be attacking, with 59 Brigade, on the day. So as not to alert the enemy, a platoon of riflemen stayed on in case the trenches were raided by the Germans.

On the 19th, just before midnight, the Norfolks moved out of the sunken road to give room for the Sherwood Foresters to enter; they would take over the right half of the attack, on the right of Argyll Road. The Norfolks moved to the left and Captain Failes' C Company went into the outpost line in No Man's Land.

The battalion would advance in the second wave with D Company on the right alongside Argyll Road, B in the centre and A on the left. They would pass through C, who would follow in support. Because they were out of sight of the enemy's trenches, each company would, in the dark, cut gaps in the wire in front of our own front line and erect bridges over every point in their sector where the white tapes for the tanks marked the line where they would smash down the enemy wire.

The left hand men of A Company would endeavour to keep in contact with 152 Brigade of the 51st Division. The Norfolks' objective was to attack and capture the Blue Line from where it crossed the Grand Ravine on the left of Ribécourt to beyond the railway station and line north of the village. They were to help the Sherwood Foresters, ensuring that the small bridges in the village were secured against any enemy who might try to demolish them.

The 1/Leicesters had trained at the village of Manin, fifteen miles west of Arras. On 14 November all the participating officers and NCOs visited a mock up of the coming battleground near Bullecourt. There were 25 officers and 639 other ranks that moved into the very congested Dessart Wood; some ten per cent of the battalion would stay there. Twenty officers and 555 other ranks moved from here to the start line near Beaucamp They would be the first wave, on the left of the 9/Suffolks, with the task of capturing the Hindenburg Front Line to the left of Argyll Road and clearing Plush Trench

By midnight of the 19th the Battalion was in position for the assault. Lieutenant PA Wrixon, commanding B Company, would have two platoons in front, No.7 on the right and No.8 on the left, touching Lancaster Road; each would have a section of three tanks from the 22nd and 24th Companies of H Battalion. They were ordered to occupy Plush Trench and, after other companies had moved through the position, support C Company in reserve.

D Company would follow without tanks on the right along Argyll Road, with A Company on the left; their objective was the enemy's third line at Unseen Support Trench. The remaining two platoons of B Company would be held in reserve specifically to reinforce the two front companies – particularly their flanks. Battalion Headquarters was in Beaucamp Support Trench, 500 yards in front of the ruined Beet Factory and just behind the British Front Line.

The 11/Essex was attached to the brigade to ensure the essential speed in achieving the capture of Flesquières Ridge.

At 6am, Lieutenant Colonel Willoughby's three Companies of H Battalion were positioned some 500 yards behind Beaucamp where the track from the hamlet ran down to Gouzeaucourt. The thirty-six tanks in three long lines faced north, each tank about thirty yards from the other. The crews had endured a long night's slow drive from Dessart Wood, each commander walking in front of his machine and guiding it along the black and white tapes. The crewmen now donned their leather helmets, shaped like a motor cyclist's, and padded to absorb the knocks they would get as they travelled. The eye holes were covered with slitted metal plates and a piece of chain mail fastened to the front to protect the chin and neck from the shards of metal always thrown off after the tank was hit. Despite the protection they offered, many of the men would discard them after a short time, as they were too uncomfortable and restricted poor vision even further.

The majority of the men had not been in action previously, though they were well aware of the hazards that lay before them, not least the risk of a petrol fire.

Just prior to setting off, 22nd Company Commander was surprised to hear and see the Tank Corps Commander, Brigadier General Hugh Elles, who informed him that he was going to go into battle in one of his tanks (*Hilda*). He took up position, with his head through the man hole at the top and remained there in that exposed position until his tank ditched at the second trench, Valley Support, on the right flank of the attack.

At 6.10am the front line of tanks, with *Hilda's* No. 1 section leading

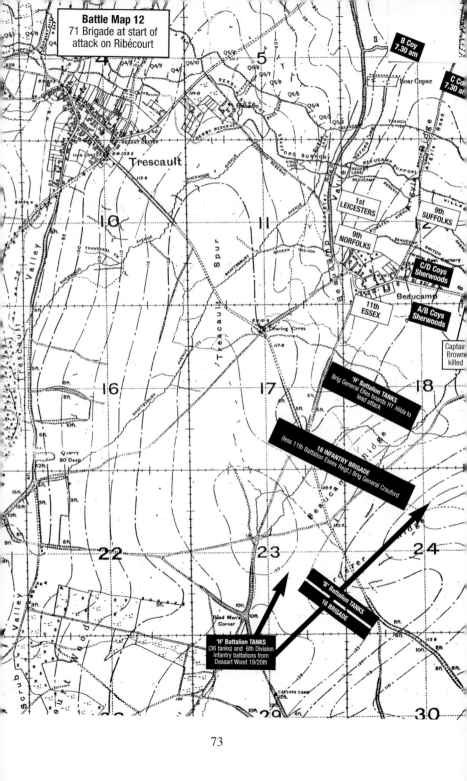

Battle Map 12
71 Brigade at start of
attack on Ribécourt

B Coy
7.30 am

C Coy
7.30 am

Boar Copse

1st
LEICESTERS

9th
SUFFOLKS

9th
NORFOLKS

C/D Coys
Sherwoods

Beaucamp

A/B Coys
Sherwoods

11th
ESSEX

Captain
Brown
killed

Charing Cross

'H' Battalion TANKS
Brig General Elles boards H1 'Hilda' to
lead attack

18 INFANTRY BRIGADE
(less 11th Battalion Essex Regt.) Brig General Crauford

'B' Battalion TANKS
16 BRIGADE

'H' Battalion TANKS
(36 tanks) and 6th Division
infantry battalions from
Dessart Wood 19/20th

Dead Man's
Corner

Trescault

the 9/Norfolks (there were six sections in all, three from the 22nd and three from the 24th companies), started to roll forward. The timing, practised many times, was perfect and as the first wave of twelve tanks, six leading the 1/ Leicesters and six leading the 9/Suffolks, arrived at the British line, the 1,000 gun barrage opened with a terrifying roar and planes from the Royal Flying Corps swept overhead to machine gun enemy trenches.

At 6.20am, following behind their six tanks, the 9/Suffolks crossed No Man's Land and quickly reached the lightly held German front line. Here Lieutenant E. Taylor was wounded after rescuing (with his batman, Private H. Smith) a tank which had caught up a barbed wire knife rest in its tread and was helpless. The enemy was completely taken by surprise and only had time to fire a few shells. Machine gun nests were destroyed by the tanks before they were able to take effective action. By 9am the battalion had seized its objective and was in touch with both flank battalions, establishing its headquarters in the original German front line. In due course C Company under Lieutenant Bryant pressed forward towards Marcoing with orders to seize the crossroads in front of the village and the bridges there over the River Escaut and the St Quentin Canal. When at about 11am the company began to advance, it was found that two platoons under Second Lieutenant A Taylor had already moved off and Second Lieutenant G Hopkins went ahead with his batman, Private A. Mingay, to try and stop them. Hopkins reached a crossroads where he found four of the enemy who surrendered. Seeing Taylor's men about 400 yards ahead to the right, he signalled to them and the two platoons closed in and joined with the rest of C Company in the advance into Marcoing. Shortly afterwards a tank arrived, as did some men from the 29th Division, who entered the village from the north. C Company then turned around and went back to Ribécourt, reaching the village and Battalion HQ after dark. The company declared that it had captured Marcoing, taken 100 prisoners and two machine guns at the cost of only two casualties. Altogether 150 prisoners and three machine guns had been taken by the Suffolks, who in turn suffering seventy casualties. These included Second Lieutenants E Taylor, W Bridewell and G Head, all wounded. Three tanks were disabled in the advance with the Suffolks: *Hengist* and *Hyacinth* from Major D Pratt's 24th Company had become stuck in one of the very wide trenches despite their fascines; and so had *Hilda*, with Elles on board. He decided to disembark and walked back to Beaucamp across the dangerous battlefield, still holding his flag and ash stick.

The 1/Leicesters had set off on the brigade's left flank at the same time, 6.20am, but due to the slowness of the six tanks some of the leading men from 7 and 8 Platoons of Lieutenant Wrixon's B Company managed to get in front. The weak enemy barrage did little damage, the tanks caught up and breached the very strong belts of barbed wire with ease and the Leicesters had no difficulty in passing through the gaps and into Plush Trench, to the great surprise of the stunned enemy, who put up very little resistance. By 9.30am all the objectives had been taken without difficulty; Battalion Headquarters was established in Unseen Trench. The Battalion was now disposed in Unseen Support Trench: D Company, plus one platoon from B on the right and A Company plus one platoon from B on the left; and in Unseen Trench there were B Company less two platoons and, in the centre, C Company. The battalion had suffered Second Lieutenant AK Purdy of B Company killed and four other ranks, with four officers and forty other ranks wounded. The battalion had captured thirty-seven prisoners, three heavy machine guns, one heavy trench mortar, three light machine guns and two aerial dart machines. The captured Germans all belonged to the 387th Regiment and had not impressed the Leicesters with the quality of their opposition. The battalion remained in the captured trench throughout the night and remained until midday on the 22nd, when 71 Brigade went into reserve a thousand yards south-west of Marcoing. The brigade occupied the Hindenburg Support Line from Couillet Wood to Premy Chapel with, from right to left the Suffolks, Leicesters, Sherwood Foresters and the Norfolks.

Twenty minutes after the 6.20am start a further six tanks crossed the line on the brigade's left between Argyll Road and Lancaster Trench. They were followed after fifty yards by the 9/Norfolks, forming part of the second wave: D Company was on the right, B Company in the centre, A Company on the left with C in support. Lieutenant Colonel Prior had arranged that, if everything went well, he would establish his headquarters in the enemy's fourth line between Unseen Trench and Ribécourt. As he would not be able to see anything of the advance because of the ridge at the top of the slope, he decided to go over with his battalion, accompanied by his intelligence officer, Lieutenant Dye, and a couple of orderlies.

Dye and I wandered well out across No Man's Land but there was no sight of friend or foe, everything was peaceful. The guns had opened up before we got halfway down the line and the leading tanks followed by the Leicesters were crossing our

*trenches and starting across No Man's Land, a wonderful sight
in the half light. Ponderous, groaning, wobbling, these engines of
war crawled, lurched their way towards the enemy's line
followed by groups of men in file. Overhead shells were pouring
over. The barrage lifted from the enemy's outpost line to the other
side of the hill where we knew that Unseen Trench was getting it
hot, but the slowness of the tanks was excruciating. Neither tanks
nor Leicesters were clear of our lines when we reached 'A'
company. I have never seen men in better fighting spirit, they all
stood up and cheered when I reached them. Our barrage had
brought a reply from the enemy's guns, causing some casualties
to our men and the Leicesters. I was, however, anxious to get on
and over the hill so as to be able to get a better view of the
'Promised Land' and be able to control the fight. In the advance
we came across Captain Blackwell with D Company; he told me
that both Lieutenants Cuthbert and Cubitt had been wounded
and that he himself was hit but could carry on. That was the last
I saw of him, for he was killed later, his first wound was a terrible
one. Nevertheless he continued to lead his Company, crossing
the Hindenburg Line before he was shot dead. As we crossed the
battlefield Lieutenant Dye was mortally wounded. After arriving
at Unseen Trench I pushed on to Unseen Support to find a
number of C Company not sure of what their next action should
be. One man shouted, 'What do we do now?' I shouted out, 'now
my lads we'll take the ruddy village', at which they laughed and
climbed out of the trench with me. Captain Failes with most of
his C Company had reached the fourth line and were in front of
me so I decided to form Battle HQ there. Captain Failes had
outstripped the other three companies and the tanks and instead
of being in support was now the front line company. Ribécourt
was immediately in front and I could see parties of the enemy
running down the streets. Our artillery was putting down a
smoke barrage on the far side of the village and several houses
were on fire. The church steeple was loopholed and made a
strongly defensible position. By this time the enemy had
recovered from his initial shock and we were being shelled and
machine gunned with accuracy. I directed Failes to push on and
take that part of the village lying on this side of the ravine and to
hold the bridge crossing it.
C Company swept on and did this in brilliant fashion, taking
many prisoners. In the meantime the tanks had negotiated the*

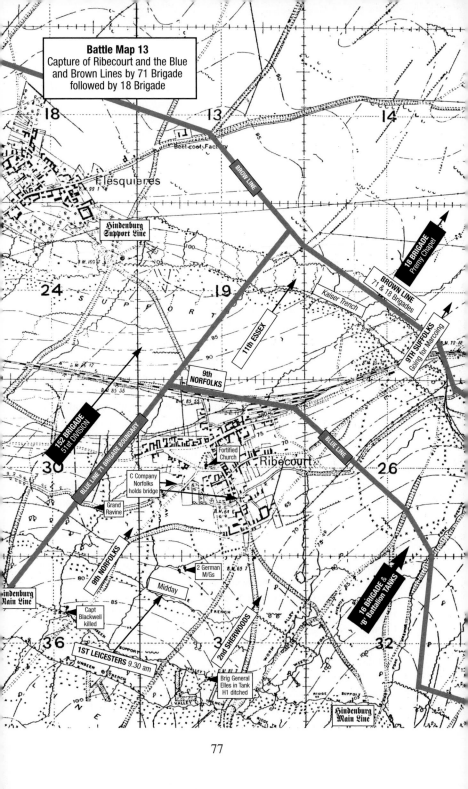

Battle Map 13
Capture of Ribecourt and the Blue and Brown Lines by 71 Brigade followed by 18 Brigade

18

13

14

Beet-root Factory

BROWN LINE

Flesquières

Hindenburg
Support Line

18 BRIGADE
Premy Chapel

BROWN LINE
71 & 18 Brigades

24

19

Kaiser Trench

9TH SUFFOLKS
Going for Marcoing

11th ESSEX

9th
NORFOLKS

152 BRIGADE
51ST DIVISION

BLUE LINE 71 BRIGADE BOUNDARY

Fortified
Church

Ribecourt

BLUE LINE

30

26

C Company
Norfolks
holds bridge

Grand Ravine

9th NORFOLKS

2 German
M/Gs

Midday

16 BRIGADE &
'B' Battalion TANKS

Hindenburg
Main Line

Capt
Blackwell
killed

3

2nd SHERWOODS

36

32

1ST LEICESTERS 9.30 am

Brig General
Elles in Tank
H1 ditched

Hindenburg
Main Line

77

formidable obstacles and were coming down the hill towards the village. It appears that as C Company opened fire and advanced seventy Germans surrendered and the Company seized the near part of the village and the two bridges over the Ravine. D Company cleared the right of the village beyond the Ravine and A the left, with B passing through C at the Ravine in the centre. C Company then dug in at the Ravine. Colonel Prior said that he was almost alone in the fourth line, Mole Trench, until he was joined by some Trench Mortar men.

B Company had then gone through and were in the village, A company was a little later on the left and I saw them making a beautiful attack on the line of houses on the left of the village supported by a Male tank with its six pounders. A Company was attacking by sectional rushes, covering the advance with rifle fire and I could not help feeling that my efforts at open warfare training whilst at Tinques had not been wasted. I could not, however, see or hear anything from D Company and was anxious about them. Cheering messages from A and B and C Companies reporting complete success began to come in, the runners arriving with broad grins and puffing German cigars. At last Captain Beezly, D Company, reported a complete success.

In fact A and D Companies had met with strong opposition and had much hand to hand fighting in clearing the village. On the left two particular troublesome machine guns were knocked out at close quarters, their crews killed by a party under Lieutenant Hancock and CSM Neale. It is estimated that the 9/Norfolks cost the enemy 80 casualties in killed and wounded and 600 prisoners. The Battalion's attack ended with the capture of Ribécourt. After the 11/Essex passed through to the left to take Kaiser Trench at the Hindenburg Support Line and on to the Brown Line, the Norfolks spent the rest of the day busy consolidating Ribécourt and putting outposts to the north of it. In the evening they took over from the 11/Essex in the Kaiser trenches where the accommodation was bad. A and D Companies had no dugouts, for the Hindenburg Support Line was nothing more than a very shallow series of trenches and pits for machine guns. The Germans had never thought that their main front line could ever be breached. Prior wrote movingly of the performance of his Battalion that day.

It would be impossible to set out all the extraordinary incidents of that glorious day, how Hancock and his Sergeant Major rushed an enemy machine gun position and settled a bet

78

as to who would kill the most Bosches. This was won by Hancock, but Sergeant Major Neale always contended that he was unduly handicapped by having to use his bayonet whilst Hancock had a revolver. How a runner from D Company, without assistance, took over seventy prisoners including a Staff Officer. How Second Lieutenant Worn, wounded in the first hundred yards of the advance, carried on with his platoon until he reached the final objective, the Railway Station, and consolidated his position. How Lieutenant Thompson of B Company, who in the darkness of the night prior to the attack had fallen down and very badly sprained his ankle, refusing to go sick and with the aid of his servant limped over the front line with his platoon and carried on until the objective was reached. How one very daring A Company man foolishly penetrated a dug out, leaving his rifle outside. Knocking down a Bosche, who thrust his pistol at his head, he seized it and harried his opponent by a vigorous application of the butt end.

Of the seven officer casualties, Captain S Blackwell, Lieutenants CG Jones and G Dye were killed; Captain Crosse and Lieutenants Cubbit, Worn and Cuthbert were wounded. Twenty-nine other ranks were killed and fifty-eight wounded. The 9/Norfolks had taken Ribécourt at a not inconsiderable cost; but it was a great contrast from the days of the Somme in 1916.

The tank commanded by Second Lieutenant F H Jackson, H45 *Hycinth*, ditched at Ribécourt.

On the right, after the 9/Suffolks had passed through them, half of the Sherwood Foresters, C and D Companies, set off with the Norfolks, the two companies behind them, A and B, who would follow in the third wave, had already been caught by the weak and scattered German artillery barrage. B Company took the brunt of it and suffered some casualties. Captain Brown, who had only recently been promoted to the rank and command of B Company, was with some men laying footboards to help D company to cross and was hit by a shell and killed. Captain Shaw, recently returned from leave and unable to take command of his A Company, was placed in command of B just as it went over the top in the second half of the Foresters' attack in the third wave. He replaced Second Lieutenant Fielding who had assumed command on Captain Brown's death.

At 9am a message was received from C Company that they had taken their first objective, the eastern edge of the Hindenburg Support trench and were advancing on the Brown Line As evidence of their progress they sent back prisoners, an officer and twenty men. They had also captured five machine guns. Unfortunately, because of the nature of the ground, their tanks had not been able to keep up with them. D Company had charged home on their objective with the bayonet, killing twelve and also taking a number of prisoners.

The advance had in general been so rapid that few messages came back. At 10.55am a report arrived, saying that D Company was consolidating the Brown Line and C Company, just behind them, was digging in at the shallow Hindenburg Support. A and B Companies would soon follow with the third wave and the 11/Essex. The 4,500 yards advance had been remarkably quick, no doubt very much assisted by the Norfolks advance; and the casualties were extremely light: one officer and eight other ranks killed and one officer and thirty other ranks wounded. The two leading companies had taken the Brown Line and captured four officers (including a Regimental Commander) and 290 NCOs and men and ten machine guns. In D Company's attack Lieutenant Edwards, the battalion's bombing officer, attacked and captured two machine guns with their crews, almost single handedly. A few days later he was hit by shell fire and seriously wounded.

A and B Companies went forward at about 8am. They had three tanks with them, but much of the work had already been done. The second half of the Sherwood Foresters made a quick advance over the many lines of trenches and piles of tangled barbed wire, killing, wounding and capturing the few Germans who were still there, after their positions had been overrun by the preceding companies. Battalion

Headquarters were established in Mole Trench, 500 yards south of Ribécourt; B Company went forward into the Hindenburg Support System at the Brown Line along with D Company. A Company had in fact gone too far forward on the track to Premy Chapel, which was 18 Brigade's objective, and runners were sent to recall it. By midday the whole battalion was in position at the Brown Line and contact had been established on the right with the 1/King's Shropshire Light Infantry (1/KSLI) of 16 Brigade.

The 11/Essex, consisting of twenty-one officers and 440 other ranks, attacked in artillery formation alongside the Sherwood Foresters and behind the tanks of the 23rd Company. Its task was to seize the Hindenburg Support System. C and D Companies led the way. The enemy fire was slight and wild and they arrived at the Main Hindenburg Line at 8.03am. At 8.30am the advance continued and twenty minutes later they learned that the Norfolks had passed through Ribécourt. At 9.45am Lieutenant Colonel Dumbell's leading companies were through the village and his Headquarters were established at the railway station. The Essex advanced on the German trenches beyond the village which was taken without difficulty. The battalion took ten officers and 200 other ranks as prisoners, along with four machine guns. In their attack they had overcome a battery of 4.2" mortars, silencing it with rifle and Lewis gun fire. The casualties were comparatively light: Captain Sydney Silver MC, commanding C Company, was killed with five other ranks; and one officer and forty-two other ranks were wounded.

Corporal G.W. Chase of the Essex wrote a telling account:

Guns captured when the 11/Essex cleared Ribécourt, 20 November 1917.

> *In the grey light of dawn we advanced under cover of tanks upon a practically deserted line. There was hardly any opposition, yet as each tank hove into view over the crest of the rise a well directed shell fired from almost point blank range disabled it.*

Corporal Chase was seeing 'E' Battalion's action on his left at Flesquières Ridge. Major Roberts, in the Transport Lines, wrote:

> *Tanks and troops moved off in the darkness, appearing like monsters in the dawn of history, guided by illuminated posts and white tapes. We at the Transport Lines became very anxious as the attack developed. Encouraging reports however came in, much to the satisfaction of the Indian Cavalry, saddled up and waiting for the orders to gallop into Cambrai. At about 2pm our spirits were raised by seeing Lieutenant Rooke leading two hundred prisoners, including a 6'3' Colonel. I went to Ribécourt that night and found all happy, Battalion Headquarters being in a cement dugout below the cellars of a large farmhouse. There I saw the 4.2' howitzer guns, two of which now stand at the entrance to Warley Barracks suitably inscribed. The next day Captain Freeman took me round different parts of the Line, many tanks were out of action and we stood and watched the fighting towards Bourlon Wood. One of these damaged tanks I saw afterwards in Trafalgar Square, being used as an office for the sale of War Saving Certificates.*

The task of 71 Brigade, to capture the right flank of the Flesquières Ridge, had been accomplished on time. It was now ready to protect the right flank of the planned 51st Highland Division's advance on Cantaing and Fontaine-Notre-Dame and its own 6th Division's advance

H30 *Hydra* had gone forward beyond Ribécourt before being hit.

on Noyelles and the vital bridge there over the St Quentin Canal.

Despite 71 Brigade's success, all was not plain sailing for the three leading battalions of 18 Brigade. Its march across the battlefield, going down to Ribécourt, was reasonably straight forward, apart from the difficulties of broken trenches and great piles of smashed barbed wire. The brigade arrived at Ribécourt shortly before 11am. The 1/West Yorks were on the right, skirting the eastern side of the village; when they topped Premy Chapel Ridge they came into the view of a German howitzer battery which promptly opened fire on them. Without hesitation the Yorkshiremen charged with the bayonet and routed them, suffering fourteen casualties and taking seventy four prisoners.

The 2/DLI came through the western side of Ribécourt but as it, too, cleared the Flesquières Ridge and the Brown Line it came under fire from Flesquières. It continued to advance and found men of the 1/6th Gordon Highlanders who were held up. The battalion pressed on north eastwards towards Premy Chapel and were then engaged by field guns. These they attacked and silenced and then further on came across a battery of six medium howitzers abandoned by their crews. When they arrived at the crossroads of Premy Chapel it was midday. They had captured eleven guns and had suffered 24 casualties.

The support battalion, the 14/DLI arrived with the loss of only seven men wounded. The prisoners taken by the brigade were survivors of the 27th Reserve Regiment, the 387th Landwehr Regiment and artillerymen of the 108th Field Regiment.

16 Brigade also did well that morning in its advance to Noyelles. The total casualties in the three brigades was fewer than 500 men but they had captured about 1,500 of the enemy. 'H' Battalion had lost four tanks due to ditching on the way down to Ribécourt, a further four by enemy action and two by ditching at the Hindenburg Support Line. It was here that *Harvester* (H4), whilst it was stopped so that one of the crew could find water for his comrades who were parched after eight hours of continuous action, was destroyed by enemy shell fire. On his return to the tank he found Captain the Hon Sir Cecil Edwards dead along with the driver and four others gravely wounded. The two who were dead were buried alongside the wreck but subsequently, because of the fluctuation of the battle, their bodies could not be found. Shortly after midday the cavalry began to arrive at Ribécourt.

Major General Mullens of the 1st Cavalry Division was told at 11.30am that Flesquières was captured and that he should take his division forward. He had advanced to Metz-en-Couture at 8.25am that morning and now understood the road from Trescault to Flesquières was fit for cavalry. His orders were to advance through the second objective. With Ribécourt secured, the cavalry came forward into the Grand Ravine only to learn that Flesquières was by no means in British hands. Two thousand men and horses now filled the low lying ground south of the village awaiting orders. In fact the Cavalry Corps Headquarters were still at Fins, seven miles away, too far away to grasp the situation of the attack. Without doubt the cavalry could have galloped around either side of Flesquières, dismounted and then attacked as infantry whilst the 51st Division was climbing the hill. However they did nothing so daring. Some of them eventually went forward to Nine Wood, Noyelles or Flot Farm, but in the evening the majority withdrew from Ribécourt. Already it was becoming obvious that the grand design of an encirclement of Cambrai would never take place.

The 51st (Highland) Division

This Scottish Territorial Division had experienced a difficult time since its arrival in France in early May 1915. It had fought at Festubert and Givenchy but was considered to be untrained, badly organized and with low morale. It suffered from having four commanders in eighteen months and when Major General Harper arrived in September 1915 they self-deprecatingly called themselves Harper's Duds, from their Divisional sign, HD.

George Harper was born in 1865 and entered the Royal Engineers in 1884. He went to France in August 1914 as part of Field Marshal French's Headquarters Staff. He was a striking figure of a man with white hair and big, black, bushy eyebrows. He immediately set about training his division and restoring morale. The division had an indifferent time in High Wood in the summer of 1916, but did extremely well at Beaumont Hamel in the dying throes of the Battle of the Somme. In 1917 it took its full share of the fighting at Arras and the Ypres Salient; in a six month period its casualties were 10,523 out of an establishment of 18,825. By now the reputation of the Highlanders was high. Harper was careful in the use of men and always sought an alternative to a frontal assault, a viewpoint which would influence his actions at Flesquières. It is true that he distrusted tanks; he appreciated their hitting power, but from unhappy experience was aware of their limitations.

Two weeks before the battle commenced his division was brought to Wailly, four miles south-west of Arras, for intensive training with tanks. Second Lieutenant Birks, commanding tank *Double Dee* III

(D27) in D Battalion, which would lead the Highland Division at Flesquières, said of this time:

> *During the training at Wailly liaison with the Highlanders consisted of simple tactical exercises by day and colossal binges by night. It is difficult to understand why so much emphasis has been laid on the lack of cooperation on the part of the 51st Division. Liaison with our battalion of the Black Watch was very close, intimate and cordial and both sides understood precisely what was required and expected.*

Several military historians have insisted that General Harper was opposed to using tanks; this is far from being true. Before the battle he issued an instruction which said, 'The tank is the primary weapon of attack', but warned that the wire cutting tanks might not advance regularly or in straight lines. He recognised the protection offered by steel plate but also the likely concentration of hostile fire upon tanks and said infantry should keep clear of that fire. He ordered that his men should not be less than 100 yards away; they should not move

Major General Harper, Commanding 51st (Highland) Division.

in 'worms' (single file behind them), as was advocated, but advance in two extended ranks. He devised his own system for the advance of the tanks, different to all other divisions at Cambrai. All three tanks in the forward sections were allocated as advanced tanks, which he called 'wire crushers', whilst the main body of tanks were 'fighters'. The 'wire crushers', moving four minutes in advance of the remainder, would deal with the enemy's support line and then move on to crush the enemy wire as much as possible. If a fascine was not needed they were to cross the Front Line trench, still in advance of the other tanks, and act similarly against the support line. Whilst the infantry advancing in long lines might have difficulty in finding gaps it was thought that great lengths of it would have been crushed by this method. The infantry were also instructed that they must not attempt to cross the wire until the enemy were engaged by the tanks. The thinking was simple: by being well behind and not bunched up in 'worms' following the tanks, casualties would be saved from the mass of fire directed on to the machines.

Commencing on the 15th the division entrained at Warlus and Beaumetz for Rocquigny, five miles south-east of Bapaume. From there the battalions went by bus and march to Metz-en-Couture, about a mile south of Havrincourt Wood, where the division's pioneer battalion, the 8/Royal Scots, and the divisional engineers had contrived to turn the ruined buildings into weatherproof accommodation under the noses of the enemy, who failed entirely to detect their work. Sufficient was made to house the whole division which finally completed its concentration on Sunday 18 November.

The division's HQ was at Ytres, three miles to the west of Metz and close to the 62nd Division's, situated at Neuville-Bourjonval, on the edge of Havrincourt Wood. At the inevitable inquest about the battle questions would be asked as to why, being so near to each other, closer cooperation was not sought between the divisions during the first morning.

The division would attack from Trescault with two brigades up. On the right was, Brigadier General HP Burn's 152 Brigade, 1/5th and 1/6th Seaforth Highlanders, 1/6th Gordons and 1/8th Argyll and Sutherland Highlanders. On the left was Brigadier General AT Beckwith's 153 Brigade, 1/6th and 1/7th Black Watch and 1/5th and 1/7th Gordon Highlanders. 154 Brigade, Brigadier General K. Buchanan's, would remain at Metz to be brought forward when required to continue the advance beyond Flesquières to Cantaing and Fontaine-Notre-Dame. 154 Brigade's battalions were the 1/4th Gordon Highlanders, 1/9th Royal Scots, 1/7th Argyll and Sutherland Highlanders and 1/4th Seaforth Highlanders.

153 Brigade would be led by thirty-five tanks from Lieutenant Colonel W. Kyngdon's 'D' Battalion on the left; and on the right, 152 Brigade by thirty-five tanks from Lieutenant Colonel Burnett's 'E' Battalion. Twenty-four from each battalion would constitute the first wave which provided a total of eight 'wire crushers'. In the attack each brigade would advance in two waves consisting of two battalions, the 1/8th Argylls on the left and the 1/5th Seaforths on the right whose neighbours were 1/Leicesters of 71 Brigade. 152 Brigade's second wave consisted of twelve tanks with 1/6th Seaforths behind the Argylls and 1/6th Gordons behind the 1/5th Seaforths.

153 Brigade would be led by the 1/5th Gordons on the left (near the West Yorkshiremen of the 62nd Division) and the 1/6th Black Watch on the right; behind them, in the second wave, also with twelve tanks, were the 1/7th Black Watch behind the Gordons and the 1/7th Gordons

following the 1/6th Black Watch. The division's frontage was 1,350 yards to start with but when it arrived at the Grand Ravine, the first objective (the Blue Line) 2,400 yards ahead, it would widen by 300 yards.

When Flesquières and the Brown Line beyond it had been taken, a further 2,700 yards, the division's front would be 2,750 yards.

Facing the division were the 84th and 27th Infantry Regiments, the latter commanded by Major Krebs; and elements of the 387th Landwehr Regiment. The enemy artillery, which would play a crucial part in the battle for the deeply entrenched, strongly barbed wired hilltop fortress which was Flesquières, consisted of six batteries from the 213th Field Regiment, 7th, 8th and 9th would particularly distinguish themselves. In addition there were also the 2nd and 8th of 108 Field Regiment of the 54th Division. The latter had already encountered French tanks and had been specially trained to deal with them.

On the 19th Major General Harper's division was ready. His affectionate nickname was 'Uncle', given to him by the division who now understood him and appreciated his concern for his men. During the day he visited them in Metz, where they had been in virtual hiding inside their billets to avoid being seen by the marauding enemy planes.

In the early hours of the 20th the attacking brigades marched into their battle positions which had been held for them by men from the 36th (Ulster) Division. These men, from 107 and 108 Brigades, would retire to the southern end of Havrincourt Wood to wait in reserve.

The 1/5th Seaforths had forty-two officers and 966 other ranks at Metz but when they arrived at Trescault and moved into their trenches

This disabled tank has become an observation platform during the advance.

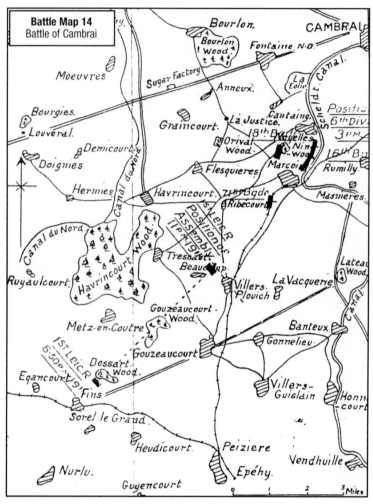

Battle Map 14
Battle of Cambrai

at 3am, the total number had been reduced by some ten per cent, left behind as a reserve. Half the battalion had gone ahead, arriving at midnight in Shaftsbury Avenue, a long communication trench leading to the front line trench Stafford Support, 1,500 yards south east of Trescault. From here they would be able at daybreak to look down the long slope to Grand Ravine. At 3.25am they were all in position and were followed by Lieutenant Colonel Robin Campbell's 1/8th Argylls going to their left into Bass Lane and Stafford Reserve. Not far behind were the two second wave battalions: the 1/6th Seaforths under Lieutenant Colonel Long positioned along the Charing Cross to

Trescault road, almost 2,000 yards behind the front line, and the 1/6th Gordons, commanded by Lieutenant Colonel the Hon. William Fraser, going into Shaftsbury Avenue behind the Seaforths. They had passed through D and E Battalions tanks as they made the short drive from the bottom corner of Havrincourt Wood. Their engines ticked over as they waited in two long lines behind the Trescault road and 152 Brigade's second wave. In due course 153 Brigade arrived, moving through the long lines of tanks and into the trench system in front of Trescault. They took up positions on either side of the track leading down to Ribécourt, in Trescault Support and in Derby Support and Reserve. The German Front Line trench (and its two lines of defensive barbed wire) was about 700 yards away. The main body of the Hindenburg Line was here at its deepest in front of the bowl, another 500 yards on. It consisted of ten lines of barbed wire and three deep trenches, the whole 800 yards wide, touching the winding Grand Ravine. From there it was 1,200 yards up the steep slope to the defences in front of Flesquières, part of the Hindenburg Support Line. Just in front of the village there was a small knoll behind the top of the ridge. Whatever was behind in the village could not be seen by the attackers. Without doubt the Highlanders would have the most formidable section of the Flesquières Ridge to conquer.

The infantry, at the request of the tank company commanders, had cut gaps in the wire and filled in parts of the trenches to help the first wave.

At 6.20am, as the stunning roar of the 1,000 gun barrage began,

F 5 *Fervent,* a male tank knocked out attacking during the attack. It is pictured here after the battle, now in the possesion of the Germans.

twelve wire crushing tanks crossed the front line and headed down the valley for their vital task, followed four minutes later by the bulk of the thirty-five fighting tanks from each battalion. On the right E Battalion's *Ella* (E 27), commanded by Second Lieutenant WS Haining, was hit by the German counter barrage, weak as it was, before it had crossed the British front line and was destroyed. Its commander and driver were killed and the other six crew members wounded. Three other tanks failed to attack because of mechanical failures. It was a chilling start for the 1/8th Argylls who were waiting close behind *Ella* for the order to advance. At Zero+15 the first wave of the leading companies of the four attacking battalions of 153 and 152 Brigades climbed out of their trenches and followed the tanks, which were then some 300 yards ahead. The infantry attack went smoothly, the German outpost line quickly falling, many Germans came out of their holes to surrender, demoralised by the terrible bombardment and the terrifying steel monsters crawling towards them spitting shells and machine gun bullets. C and D companies of the 1/5th Seaforths on the right flank captured twelve officers and 200 other ranks, with four machine guns, even though two more tanks had failed due to mechanical problems. When A and B Companies left an hour later, apart from a few light shells falling, they had no casualties and minimal resistance. In fact throughout the day the 1/5th escaped off extremely lightly, with only twenty wounded and four killed. After they had crossed the Grand Ravine shortly after 9.30am a machine gun firing from Ribécourt on the right was troublesome. Lance Corporal Robert McBeath was sent with a small patrol to reconnoitre the problem and found that there was still a large machine gun post in action. After shooting one of the crew dead he advanced, supported by a tank who had seen his action, and captured the headquarters of a German battalion almost single handedly. He killed three and took thirty-two prisoners, including two officers and five machine guns. He was awarded the Victoria Cross.

Lance Corporal
Robert McBeath VC.

At Zero+90 the 1/6th Seaforths and 1/6th Gordons advanced in the second wave, arriving in the Grand Ravine at about 8.30am without much trouble. The 1/8th Argylls had a more difficult time going through the edge of Femy Wood, particularly true for the tanks because of the stumps and felled trees. Nevertheless the battalion reached the Grand Ravine shortly after 8am with only a few casualties. The enemy resisted strongly at Triangle Wood, just beyond the second row of trenches in the Hindenburg Main Line, where the Argylls were helped by two of E Battalion's tanks. Lieutenant Colonel Campbell's battalion had suffered one officer killed and two wounded and nine other ranks killed and forty wounded. The brigade had now crossed the Blue Line.

On the left of the division 153 Brigade had started out behind the thirty-five tanks after the twelve wire crushers of D Battalion had done their job. The 1/5th Gordons on the left and Lieutenant Colonel Neil Campbell's 1/6th Black Watch on the right were some hundreds of yards behind them. Campbell had shown remarkable foresight because at 6am on the 19th he had brought his HQ with C Company and half of B, six platoons in total, into the trenches north-east of Trescault, relieving the Royal Irish Rifles, so that his men could learn the lie of the land and the various landmarks. Lieutenant HS Graves had also gone out in the night of the 19/20th to lay out white tapes at right angles to the advance, placing flags to show the platoons' flanks. He would be seriously wounded later in the day.

The German Outpost Line quickly fell as it had done on the right, the enemy showing little resistance after their first terrible hour of shelling and advancing tanks. However when the tanks reached the first part of the Hindenburg Main Line, shortly after 7am, the German resistance stiffened. Here the trenches had been dug very wide and deep; the fascines could not fill them in and the tanks ran into trouble. Four tanks of the leading line immediately became stuck, two more ditched, three ran out of ammunition and had to return and seven others developed mechanical trouble. Only one in front of the 1/5th Gordons on the left, managed to cross the second trench of the Hindenburg

The village of Ribécourt two hours after its capture. German prisoners are being gathered to be marched to the rear.

Main Line. Lieutenant Colonel McTaggart's men had so far had a great day, they had captured 400 enemy with only six men killed and four officers and fifty-two men wounded.

The 1/6th Black Watch on the right of 153 Brigade, moving 150 yards behind the tanks, overran the Outpost Line, taking thirty terrified prisoners with very little loss, As soon as the battalion's first wave had taken the Outpost Line, the second half of the battalion advanced about an hour after Zero to be held up by a machine gun post that the tanks had missed. Sergeant NS Teele crawled forward and with a bomb settled the machine gun team and captured the gun. At 7.45am the Black Watch were well into the Hindenburg Main Line, capturing eighty of the enemy. So far all had gone well, the tanks doing all that was asked of them but, at Mole Trench, the last in the main defences which ran behind the whole length of the German Line from east of Ribécourt, they were held up by two machine gun posts. Sergeant Loftus and Corporal Simpson wiped them out with bombs. On the left they were also held up by uncut barbed wire but Captain Brown attracted the attention of three tanks which quickly smashed the wire, allowing the Black Watch to capture Mole Trench and take many prisoners. Arriving at Grand Ravine they came under intense machine

Men of the 1/4th Gordon Highlanders moving forward, 20 November.

gun fire but Private Peddle crawled forward up to the enemy post and with rifle and grenades killed five and wounded two more of the garrison, which now collapsed. Once again a tank came to help and very soon the whole length of the Ravine was cleared. Six officers and 100 other ranks surrendered whilst the casualties of the battalion in the 5,000 yards advance had been incredibly light. One officer was killed, Lieutenant C McNicoll, and two wounded, eight other ranks killed and thirty-four wounded.

The whole brigade had arrived at the Grand Ravine just after 9am and set about clearing the enemy out of their dugouts. Casualties were under 120 and they had captured 600 Germans from five battalions of defenders, mainly from the 387th and 84th Regiments. Major Hofmeister, commanding the 84th, had been surprised by the attack. His headquarters were in a block house in the Support Line, east of Flesquières. He sent *Hauptmann* Willie of I Battalion forward to hold the line, but it soon fell to the 1/6th Seaforths.

The attack of the Highland Division now halted. The 1/7th Gordon Highlanders and the 1/7th Black Watch came through to carry on the brigade's assault on Flesquières. Lieutenant Colonel HH Sutherland had returned to the 1/7th Black Watch only in November after some time in temporary command of the brigade. He had shown his knowledge of battle conditions when, bringing forward his advance

party to view the battlefield on the 19th, they discarded their Highland kit and donned ordinary khaki uniforms to disguise their arrival.

The bombardment of the Hindenburg Support Line was continued. It was not scheduled to lift until 9.30am and until then the front face of the Line and Flesquières was smothered in the smoke barrage. 'Uncle' Harper now left his two brigades rest. He would be criticised severely for this later – for not carrying on with the attack and not bringing 154 Brigade into the battle – but he knew the barrage and the smoke must lift before he could commit more men. In any case the tanks could simply not see their way forward. They would be invaluable because of the maze of tangled barbed wire that had not yet been breached. On the other hand, perhaps he should have remembered Haig's order for speed and the vital capture of Bourlon that day.

In the dark hours of the following morning he did send 154 Brigade forward to continue the advance after Flesquières had fallen.

In the Grand Ravine the tank crews dismounted, breathing clean air, refuelling and replenishing their machines. The infantry cleared the enemy dugouts and in some cases went on a looting spree, grabbing cigars, brandy, trophies and whatever else took their fancy.

At 9.30am the two brigades advanced to the Hindenburg Support Line, running down from the north and the 62nd Yorkshire (West Riding) Division's sector. A double line of deep trenches and much barbed wire ran across the front of Flesquières, covering the ridge in front of the village and then curving south-east to Ribécourt. Unseen beyond the ridge were German batteries waiting for the tanks which they knew would soon be in their open sights.

153 Brigade on the left would head for the Cambrai-Bapaume railway line, then Cemetery Trench, Flesquières Trench and the left side of the village. They would have with them ten tanks from D Battalion's second wave and the eight surviving tanks from the first. 152 Brigade on the right, led by the 1/6th Seaforths and the 1/6th Gordons, would follow twelve tanks from E Battalion and the twenty left from the earlier attack. They hoped to flank the village and enter it round the wood of Flesquières Chateau Farm (mistakenly called on British trench maps simply Flesquières Chateau), with its high and solid brick wall behind which were a number of purpose built cylindrical steel machine gun positions. The Brown Line was only 1,000 yards further.

At this time, informed that the road from Trescault to Flesquières was open, the 2nd Cavalry Brigade from the 1st Cavalry Division, the 4th and 5th Dragoon Guards, started out from Fins. At 11am advanced Brigade Headquarters were opened at the ruins of Bilhem Farm on the eastern edge of Trescault; one squadron of the 4th was ordered forward. It was soon obvious that the road was not clear. It did receive orders to take part in an operation to clear Flesquières but these arrived too late and in any case they wanted to advance on Marcoing and Nine Wood that afternoon.

It was drizzling and the day, which had started with a clear sky, was now wet, dark and miserable. With the lifting of the artillery barrage the two battalions of 152 Brigade, the Seaforths and the Gordons, began to climb the hill. The tanks from E Battalion were perhaps three hundred yards ahead, much too far for the essential support they might need when approaching the fortress. As it turned out it would not have mattered had the gap been halved. The village alone held about 600 German infantry men, most of whom were hidden in the cellars. They knew how to deal with tanks; bundles of grenades were prepared to throw beneath them to blow off the tracks.

Shortly before 10am, Lieutenant Colonel Fraser's 1/6th Gordons were at the railway embankment, 300 yards in front of a shallow German trench, the outpost line of the Hindenburg Support System. The twelve tanks of the 13th Company of E Battalion were not far ahead and were about to enter the lines of barbed wire of the Hindenburg Support, as were those of the 15th Tank Company. The Highlanders had a perfect view of the disaster, a disaster blamed on Harper's order to his men to keep well away from the tanks. This view does not appear to be justified.

The tanks advanced 'line ahead', not in their usual 'abreast' manner, no doubt because of the many great shell holes in the fields on either side of the sunken lane which ran north to the south-eastern edge of Flesquières Chateau Farm's wood. The trees there had been greatly thinned, both by the German defenders and the recent bombardment. At the top of the lane, which in fact was the track going to Cantaing, passing Flesquières eastern side, there was a ridge. On the other side of the track running from Ribécourt to Flesquières there was a thin line of battered trees shielding the large depression of an open field.

In the middle of the field, unseen by any British aircraft, which had left the scene much earlier when the guns were hidden below ground, was Number 8 Battery of the 108th Field Artillery Regiment. Major Hofmeister, commanding the defence of village (and later killed there), ordered *Leutenant* Ruppel to get his four 77mm field guns of 8 Battery out of their pits and prepare to take on the tanks which were bound to come up the hill, and destroy them before they could crush the wire. The German artillery opened fire at 500 yards as the first tank came into view. Six other tanks of Major Montgomery's 15th Company had closed up, almost nose to tail, and now appeared in the field gunners' sights; within minutes seven tanks were brought to a halt, five of them in flames. The barbed wire had not been breached. Further to the right, of the twenty tanks attacking in line abreast, eleven were also knocked out. It was an awful day for Lieutenant Colonel Burnett's E Battalion. The morning had been bad enough but now, shortly before dusk (at 4.20pm) his total losses in tanks was twenty-eight, eighteen by enemy action, five of them burnt out. He had lost 115 officers and men with another thirty-five wounded but still at duty, a percentage total greater than any of the infantry battalions involved on the right flank of the division.

With tanks on fire in front of them and the wounded crew struggling to escape, the 1/6th Gordons resumed their advance. German machine gunners and riflemen manned the trenches in front of them and their initial burst of fire at the Gordons brought sixty men down. With the massive wire defences still intact, no more tanks to sweep it away, the weather closing in and darkness falling, Lieutenant Colonel Fraser had no other recourse but to dig in and wait. It would be the following morning before they entered Flesquières.

There are two legends about the fight on the right flank at Flesquières. The first is that the Gordons were reluctant to push forward hard and owing to their divisional commander's instructions were too far behind the tanks for the support they needed. The infantry, so the argument goes, could have overcome the German gunners by rifle and Lewis gun fire, thus saving the tanks from catastrophe and could then have followed them into the village. This is fanciful criticism. The wire was not breached, the tanks had been brutally stopped and it was impossible for the Gordons to have gone forward. Furthermore, the night was upon them and 'Uncle' Harper wisely waited for daylight. Certainly there were not many Germans left in Flesquières but they were brave and determined reinforcements could not be far away. A black night was no place for tanks, the crew's visibility was bad enough in broad daylight.

The other story relates to a German artillery officer at the battery of guns which did so much damage. The story was that a single German officer, *Unteroffizier* Theodore Krüger, remained at his gun when all the rest of his crew were dead, knocking out five tanks and fighting on until this hero was killed. It became headlines in Britain, and perhaps a simple rumour was enlarged by media hype. At the time, and indeed long after the war, the Germans knew nothing of this. The basis of the story seems to lie in the fact that when the battery was taken there was only one identifiable body. Under Hitler the story was seized upon and a statue was raised in Cologne showing a hatless officer with his arm raised at a field gun.

On the left of the 1/6th Gordons were the 1/6th Seaforths. After the barrage lifted off the hill they went forward with the Gordons, about 200 yards behind seven tanks of 15 Company: *Emperor, Edinburgh, Endurance, Exquisite, Euryalius, Egypt* and *Eileen.* Advancing on the left and centre of the Seaforths they crossed and sat astride the first trench. On the right the tanks had not come up so the wire was not cut. The first double wave of A Company succeeded in entering the trench with only three casualties. The tanks moved over to the right and became part of the disaster there. C Company, on the right, was not so lucky, managing to push through into the trench where the wire had been cut but suffering several casualties. There

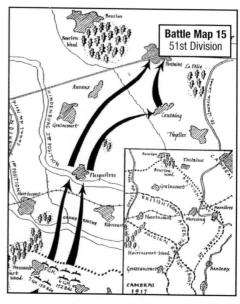

was some hard fighting but a lot of Germans were killed, many prisoners taken and the trench was captured. Then the Company endeavoured to get in touch with the Gordons on the right by advancing over the top of the trench. After fifty yards it became impossible, the enemy fire was too fierce from Flesquières Trench but a bombing block was established. It was near here that the Seaforths uncovered a deep dugout, in fact an observation post. The garrison commander, *Hauptmann* Willie, at first refused to surrender but finally did so when his telephone line was cut and he could no longer report to Major Hofmeister. Two officers and eighteen men surrendered. The CO of the Seaforths' report noted:

> *The tanks which crossed in the centre of the battalion front had made excellent progress and done splendid work, when several of them were knocked out by direct hits as they proceeded to Flesquières Trench and the others, running short of petrol, could not proceed further. Heavy machine gun fire was now encountered from the houses in the village and from the trench in the wood. On the left touch was established with the 1/7th Gordons but on the right the 1/6th Gordons were held by the wire and the heavy machine gun fire. An attempt was made by our second wave to push forward up to Flesquières Trench; except at one point this was impossible, in spite of determined efforts by men and great gallantry by the officers, only one succeeding in*

reaching the trench.

This officer, Lieutenant Grant, led his men forward along a communication trench, Ravine Alley, with tremendous dash and gallantry. Lieutenant Grant bayoneted a good many of the enemy himself and with one man left from his platoon was about to enter Flesquières Trench, having just jumped out of the communication trench where he had done so well, when he and his orderly were fatally shot. This attempt cost many lives, only one officer in each of the two leading companies was left, both junior lieutenants. I now pushed forward myself and quickly took in the whole situation and then proceeded to reorganise both companies. The enemy fire was intense; the place seemed alive with machine guns. Tanks came up on our left but, as they had no petrol, could not go on. However they opened fire with their Lewis guns and six pounders. I ordered an advance under this covering fire and got the men forward but the tanks had ceased firing and again there was a tremendous fusillade of machine gun fire from the village. After severe fighting we gained a foothold in Flesquières Trench, with our right resting on the Flesquières-Ribécourt road and our left three hundred yards round the south east corner of the village. From this trench we made two determined attempts to attack the village by rushes, covering the attack with heavy rifle and Lewis gun fire. This was unsuccessful, for the enemy machine gun fire poured upon us from behind the high walls and houses in the eastern side of the village.

Later in the afternoon seven tanks from 14 Company came up, six of which entered the village. One of them was E40, *Edward II*, commanded by Second Lieutenant W.R. Bion. His tank was soon destroyed. However, he, with two of his men, Privates W Richardson and GE Bell, removed a Lewis gun from the tank and commandeered a German machine gun and joined A Company of the Seaforths in attacking the enemy. His gallantry was extraordinary and at one time climbed back on to his ruined tank to get a better shot at an enemy post. Whilst talking to him the commander of the Seaforths A Company, Captain Edwards, was killed. Bion remained with the Seaforths in their battle in the streets of the village. He later received the DSO and his two men the Military Medal.

The Seaforths CO wrote:

I ordered two platoons to attack through the wood and two more to enter the village. This attack was supported by Stokes

Mortars and rifle grenades. The first party was driven back but the second entered the village and pushed through. Unfortunately the tanks went back, without rendering the required assistance. We did our best to establish a series of posts round the village but, as my left flank was exposed and we were being fired on at front and behind from all over the village, I was compelled to withdraw my men. It was now quite dark and I made dispositions for guarding both my flanks and holding on to Flesquières Trench. From it I made a show of strength by keeping up incessant rifle and Lewis gun fire on the village. As Flesquières was the key to the situation I wrote to the OC 1/7th Gordons, suggesting we made a joint attack at 10pm with a view to establishing an outpost line beyond the village. Unfortunately he was not at his headquarters when my message was received there but he was later. He replied saying that the night was too dark for the attempt. Nothing was therefore done.

My casualties were six officers and twenty other ranks killed, three officers and forty-three other ranks wounded with three missing. We had captured three hundred and five enemy and I estimated we had killed at least fifty Germans.

The drizzling rain had continued all day and at dusk 152 Brigade's effort came to a close. It had ended unsatisfactorily but the battalions and tanks had done all they could in the short, winter day. The infantry had simply not been able to get to the tanks quickly enough when they had entered Flesquières. The resolute Germans, hidden in the houses and aided by the darkening skies, had attacked at close range and the tanks, whose crews visibility was reduced to practically nothing, were

Flesquières Church after 20 November 1917.

powerless in the narrow winding streets. All they could do was fire into the buildings but most of the enemy were safely below ground. The infantry's report that the tanks had left them behind in the village gave the lie that they had been too far behind because of their tactics. Rather it was German opposition and barbed wire, coupled with the fatigue of the tank crews and the limitations of the machines in the dark that was the cause.

Of course there were other factors that are rarely mentioned. One was the early exit of the Royal Flying Corps from the battle. Another was the field artillery's inability to get loose from the mass barrage plan and shell the enemy artillery at and behind Flesquières. Finally, and despite the efforts of the artillery observation officers and the Royal Engineer surveyors, the 1,000 gun barrage had not fallen heavily enough on the Hindenburg Support System – the mass of barbed wire in front of Flesquières had been hardly touched.

Happily the brigade's casualties had been light and far less than anticipated. In total they were not more than 300.

153 Brigade, on the left of the division's attack, were led up the hill by D Battalion to attack the left centre and western end of Flesquières. Within 300 yards the two attacking infantry battalions, the 1/7th Black Watch on the left and the 1/7th Gordons on the right, had crossed the Blue Line. There were only twenty fresh tanks, ten from Major ROC Ward's 12th Company, and eight survivors from the battle through the Hindenburg Main Line. A long switch trench, Cemetery Alley, which it joined Chapel Trench in the 62nd Division's sector came across the slope, over the railway embankment then came in front of the cemetery and joined Flesquières Trench at the south-west corner of Flesquières and the Hindenburg Support Line. It was strongly held, particularly after the Germans had seen the West Yorks storming of Havrincourt's eastern side. The tanks and the Black Watch were having a hard time of it.

Initially 153 Brigade's advance up the slope to the Hindenburg

Chateau de Flesquières when in use by the Germans and before its destruction.

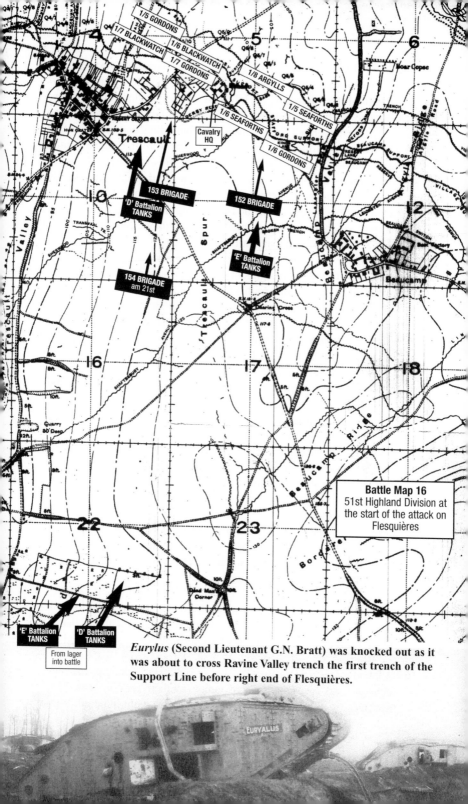

Battle Map 16
51st Highland Division at
the start of the attack on
Flesquières

Eurylus (Second Lieutenant G.N. Bratt) was knocked out as it
was about to cross Ravine Valley trench the first trench of the
Support Line before right end of Flesquières.

Support Line and Flesquières seemed to be a complete surprise to the enemy, being met only with a weak barrage. Chapel Trench, 500 yards forward of the Ravine, on the left flank of the Division was taken by C Company of the 1/7th Black Watch and the Gordons relieved them. Carrying on, Colonel Sutherland's men found they had lost their tanks and were met with heavy machine gun fire from the railway cutting three hundred yards ahead. In spite of this, Captain Beveridge, commanding C Company, gained the cutting and at Cemetery Alley, a trench that had once been a track from Havrincourt to Flesquières running across his front into the Hindenburg Support System, took two hundred prisoners. He reached the formidable Support Line by 10.45am. Here his company suffered a set back. In crossing the ridge to reach the line the surviving tanks came under fire of a German battery from the 108th Regiment, and eight of them were knocked out by direct hits. In addition to this they were unable to break through the thick belts of barbed wire and the attacking Highlanders were swept with machine gun fire. In fact one tank had managed to enter the village, getting to the eastern end until it too was knocked out. D Battalion's casualties were terrible: in total it had lost twenty tanks, with nineteen crew members killed and eighty-six wounded. Major ROC Ward, commanding the 12th Company, was the most senior officer of the four killed. Major E Harris, commanding the 10th Company, was seriously wounded and taken prisoner.

In the afternoon the Black Watch reached Flesquières Trench, but no further advance was possible. In this fighting Second Lieutenant Clark's platoon was held up by machine gun fire and his Lewis gun section all became casualties. He then continued to work the gun, forcing the enemy to retire, but was killed about that point. On the right Lieutenant Colonel A Long's 1/7th Gordons also advanced up the slope alongside the Black Watch. However, in front the wire was still thick. Long thought he could advance if he could have artillery and tank support but was told to hold his hand. It was dark and the advice to wait until the morning was sound.

At dusk the 51st (Highland) Division's attempt to take the centre of the Havrincourt-Flesquières Ridge on 20 November came to a halt. The division was virtually at the bottom of a salient with the flanking divisions successful. But, until Flesquières was taken the grand plan for Bourlon was in jeopardy. 'Uncle Harper' would capture it the following day very easily – indeed at no cost. So far his casualties, including the two battalions of tanks (in their case in men, if not machines', had been incredibly light, less than eight hundred. Within

Two knocked out British tanks *Egypt II*, E17 (Second Lieutenant G. Test, killed) and *Eurylus* (Second Lieutenant G.N. Bratt). These tanks were operating in support of the 51st Highland Division.

German 77mm gun crew in action against tanks. The field gun, properly handled, was remarkably effective against the slow moving tanks.

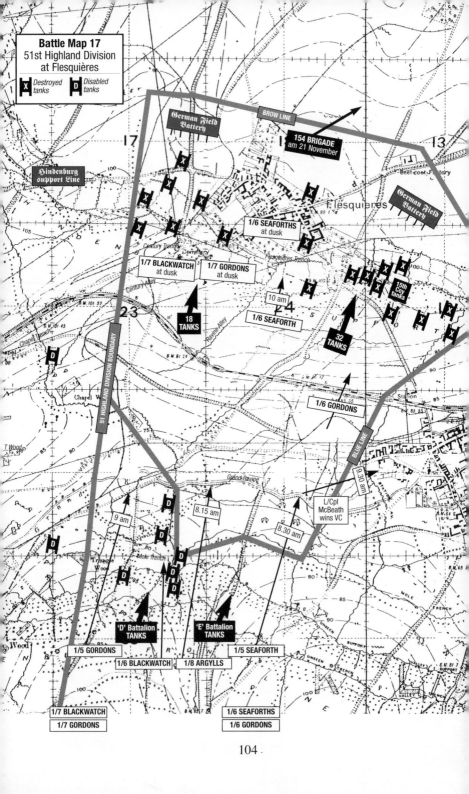

Battle Map 17
51st Highland Division
at Flesquières

X Destroyed tanks **D** Disabled tanks

German Field Battery

BROW LINE

154 BRIGADE
am 21 November

17

13

Hindenburg support Line

German Field Battery

Flesquieres

1/6 SEAFORTHS
at dusk

Century Trench   Cemetery

Flesquieres Trench

1/7 BLACKWATCH
at dusk

1/7 GORDONS
at dusk

Century Alley

23

10 am

1/6 SEAFORTH

15th Coy tanks

18 TANKS

Ravine Alley

Chapel Trench

32 TANKS

1/6 GORDONS

51st HIGHLAND DIVISION BOUNDARY

Chapel Wood Trench

Station

T Wood

BLUE LINE

Grand Ravine

9 am

8.15 am

8.30 am

L/Cpl McBeath wins VC

9.30 am

D TANKS

Mole Trench

Triangle Wood

'D' Battalion TANKS

'E' Battalion TANKS

MOLE TRENCH

1/5 GORDONS

1/6 BLACKWATCH

1/8 ARGYLLS

1/5 SEAFORTH

Wood

UNSEEN TRENCH

VALLEY

1/7 BLACKWATCH

1/7 GORDONS

1/6 SEAFORTHS

1/6 GORDONS

the next three days this would increase to 1,570. His Division had captured 1,548 unwounded prisoners, and 5,785 German officers and men were reported missing in the fighting along the battle front at the end of the day.

Major General Harper was reasonably happy early on the morning of the 21st. In fact when the battle for Cambrai was over much of the adverse criticism of his performance was nullified. Certainly his flanking divisions had achieved their objectives, an advance of astonishing length, but to his right the battle for the canal bridges had failed. However, the advance to them was of an unparalleled distance, so much so that the journalists and the population, thirsty for a victory, lauded the action and church bells rang out that morning all over Great Britain.

Of all the unfortunate calculations made in the planning, perhaps two stand out. The first was simply fatigue; 'Uncle' Harper understood this better than most. Whether or not the infantry of any of the three divisions involved with Flesquières Ridge could have continued to Bourlon. After their long hard day will always be disputed. Not only fatigue was an issue, of course, but also the quality of the German defence and the continuing lack of flexibility – mainly for logistical reasons, of the artillery. The second was the limitations of the tank. Every member of the Corps was absolutely tired out and its losses in both men and tanks had been severe. Three hundred and seventy-eight tanks had been available for the whole length of the attack in both III and IV Corps but not all were used. Of those that were, 179 were put out of action: sixty-five by direct hits and 114 were 'ditched' or halted by mechanical troubles. Slow and cumbersome as the tank was, it had done a superb job in eliminating barbed wire; but its vulnerability to artillery and armour piercing rifle fire was cruelly exposed. Elles would work to rectify the problems in the months to come.

At 7.15pm on the 20th Major General Harper issued orders that Flesquières would be captured by a dawn attack the following day. This was to be followed by an advance of 154 Brigade. It would move through Flesquières and continue its advance to the Premy Chapel-Graincourt road which would become its start line. At 10am it would assault the Cantaing and Bourlon trenches as an intermediate objective, with the village of Fontaine-Notre-Dame as the final one. Some tanks

Major Krebs, who commanded the German defence of Flesquières.

Brigand II B24, knocked out on 21 November, when supporting the Highland Division.

would be available before the attack on Cantaing; eventually six appeared from H Battalion.

Major Krebs, now commanding the defence of Flesquières, was also relatively content. Certainly he had been astonished at the ease and speed with which the British had succeeded in breaching the much vaunted Hindenburg Main Line, something that he and all his superiors had thought almost impossible, and certainly not achievable in so short a space of time. He was delighted with his artillery's performance against the tank and had learned a lot from it. He understood why Ludendorff had little time for them.

Meanwhile, Crown Prince Rupprecht of Bavaria, commanding the Northern Army Group, of which the Second Army formed the left flank, noted the deep penetration of positions which, being of special strength were thinly manned by troops of indifferent quality and who enjoyed relatively little artillery support. He was surprised at the speed of the tanks and still more at the ease with which they had negotiated the formidable barbed wire. During the morning of the 20th, as the situation grew worse, reinforcements were hurriedly summoned and began their advance towards the Cambrai front.

The 52nd Reserve Regiment was ordered to hold Flesquières, but time was needed to get them there. On in the evening of the 20th Krebs was told that reinforcements could not get to him until sometime on the 21st. He knew that Flesquières was almost cut off and that the roads from it to the fortified villages of Cantaing and Fontaine-Notre-Dame

106

would soon be impassable. He had to get out now or his little command would be eliminated. By 10pm his front was silent. Very quietly, at about midnight and leaving German and British dead where they had fallen amongst the still blazing tanks, he and his gallant band slipped away.

Very late on the 20th and in the early hours of the 21st the Highland Division's artillery came forward, taking up positions about Trescault for the attack on Flesquières. At about the same time 154 Brigade, with Lieutenant Colonel JA Durie's 1/7th Argylls on the left and the 1/4th Gordon Highlanders on the right leading the formation, moved into the old British front line trenches. Lieutenant Colonel Rowbotham would be awarded the DSO for leading his Gordons into the attack on Cantaing on his horse. Behind them, leaving Metz-en-Couture at 4am, came the 1/4th Seaforths (Lieutenant Colonel Unthank) and 1/9th Royal Scots (Lieutenant Colonel McMicking). The Royal Scots would have a remarkably easy day.

In the quiet of the night patrols were sent out, penetrating the few gaps in the wire, cutting through it as necessary and searching for defenders. Zero hour would be at 6.45am for both 153 and 152 Brigades. At 2am the 1/7th Black Watch reported that the village was empty. The advance into Flesquières was now brought forward and by 6am the four leading battalions were occupying the Brown Line, 500 yards north of the village, their target of the previous day. The advance

The remains of *Hypatia* (H48 Second Lieutenant Hancock), with Fontaine in the background.

had not been totally trouble free. Anneux, 3,000 yards to the north, had not yet been taken by 186 Brigade and long range machine gun fire harassed the attack.

Flesquières Ridge was finally British and by Great War standards at minimal cost in lives. This now almost had a platform 7,000 yards wide to launch his next operation. The last section came a few hours later when Cantaing fell.

Flesquières was about 5,000 yards from Bourlon Wood and the main road. Byng's attack here would fall between Fontaine on the right and Anneux on the left. The land between the ridge and Bourlon Hill was almost bereft of trees and flat with a slight convex rise in the middle. By 27 November he was to capture about sixty square miles of German held territory. The German High Command was, quite naturally, determined to regain it.

By the 27th Byng's front was 20,000 yards if the curvature of the line is allowed for. Third Army had pushed through the Hindenburg Line to a depth of more than 10,000 yards. In the battle, the Third Army had employed fifteen infantry and five cavalry divisions, along with three brigades of tanks. A full account of the German counter attack can be found in *Cambrai: The Right Hook* and *Cambrai: Bourlon Wood* in this series.

Edward II, (E40 Second Lieutenant W.R. Bion), knocked out attacking at Flesquières.

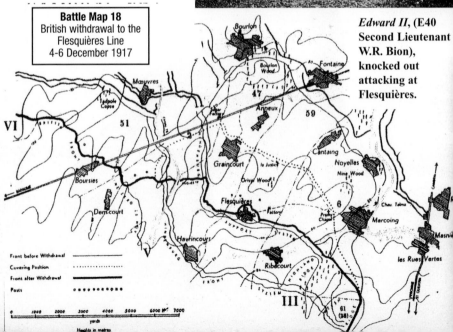

Battle Map 18
British withdrawal to the Flesquières Line
4-6 December 1917

Front before Withdrawal ————
Covering Position ············
Front after Withdrawal ▬▬▬▬
Posts •••••••••••

Chapter Three

FLESQUIÈRES: THE SALIENT, DECEMBER 1917

On 2 December 1917 Haig discussed with Kiggel, his Chief of the General Staff, the question of withdrawing from the Marcoing-Bourlon Salient now that the Third Army had been thrown on the defensive by the German Counter Stroke, Crown Prince Rupprecht's plan to strike in the south and roll up the British and then destroy them with a hammer blow coming from the north, out of Bourlon.

Fresh German attacks were expected and the British divisions which were arriving to relieve the tired troops holding the British line were themselves in need of reinforcements and rest. They had been in reserve areas after battles elsewhere but that rest was cut short by the needs of Cambrai. The prospect for everybody was grim, winter had arrived and the ground had already become frozen hard.

Haig also expected that in the spring Ludendorff would launch a huge offensive – German options were limited because of the arrival of the Americans in force no later than 1919 and they had a golden opportunity with the ending of the war in Russia. In Albert on the morning of the 3rd he discussed with Byng the selection of a good winter line. Byng advised that he would need at least two extra divisions if the Marcoing-Bourlon Salient was to be held permanently. He had selected a rear line which more or less coincided with the Hindenburg Support Line and included the defences at Flesquières, which were strong and suitable. This would not require the

Awaiting the pouring of concrete, uncompleted German defences at Flesquières.

commitment of any more troops and was, in all ways, a preferable line to hold.

It was quiet on the morning of the 4th, apart from desultory artillery fire and an apparent concentration of the enemy four miles to the left of Bourlon, at Moeuvres. At 9.30am the order to withdraw from Marcoing, Nine Wood, Noyelles, Cantaing, Bourlon Wood, Anneux and Graincourt was issued, the troops to fall back to Flesquières, high on its ridge, and in front of Ribécourt, two miles below. The final withdrawal would commence at 3am on the 5th; the main body of infantry and artillery would already have come away, to be west of a line from Premy Chapel, La Justice, Graincourt, to the Sugar Factory on the Bapaume Road. This line, 2,000 yards forward of the main line at Flesquières, was called the Yellow Line. It was the covering position until all were behind the main line. This covering position was to be held until the night of the 5/6 December at the earliest, to give time for the main line to be worked on. There was much to do with the old German trenches, there was no barbed wire at all facing the expected attackers, or trenches in front of Flesquières. Any derelict tanks that could be of use to the enemy in front of the line were destroyed.

There were three divisions in the line about Flesquières, roughly following the old Brown Line of the attack on the 20th. On the right, for a thousand yards from Premy Chapel, was the 6th Division, which had never left the battle front. 71 Brigade held the covering position. On the left, at Graincourt, the 47th (2nd London) Division would hold on until it withdrew into the Main Line, near the empty Canal du Nord, leaving Graincourt to the enemy. At Flesquières was the 59th (2nd North Midland) Division, consisting of 176, 177 and 178 Brigades.

On the evening of the 4th Lieutenant Colonel Martyn, commanding the 2/7th Sherwood Foresters (the 'Robin Hoods'), 178 Brigade, sent for all Company and Specialist officers and told them that special orders would come that night which he could not yet divulge. For the remaining few minutes of daylight they were to examine the ground and see what rapid steps could be taken should it become the last line of defence. When the orders came they were startling. Two companies of the 2/4th Lincolns (177 Brigade) with the 2/7th Foresters would form an outpost line where they then were. The present position would be evacuated and by 5am the sunken road would be the front line. This sunken road ran from the bottom south east corner of Graincourt in a shallow, north facing arc, down to the road from Cantaing to Flesquières, a distance of 2,000 yards. In the middle was a cross roads on the Cantaing road, near a large, ruined farm house called La Justice.

The Germans had previously greatly strengthened it with concrete and whilst the British were at Bourlon had used it as a Casualty Clearing Station. In front of the sunken road the open, treeless land was convex; there was a low rise which would dramatically reduce the field of fire. The whole of Flesquières, moreover, was overlooked by Fontaine-Notre-Dame on its ridge 2,500 yards to the north east. There was no cover at all along the sunken road. It did, however, contain a number of German dugouts and all were in good condition, one with several rooms and what had once been a telegraph centre being used as a Battalion Headquarters. The road here had a very steep bank and even now a relay stretcher party from the Londoners of the 47th Division were treating badly wounded men at La Justice, mostly gassed, reeling like drunken men and partially blind. Bourlon Wood had received 16,000 German phosgene gas shells during the fighting there.

Lieutenant Colonel Martyn was placed in command of the new Outpost Line, 2,000 yards in front of Flesquières. He formed the troops that would man it into three groups. The right group was formed of A and D Companies of the Sherwood Foresters. The centre group was to be formed from the Lincolns, who at this stage in proceedings were still getting out of the Bourlon area. The left group consisted of the other two companies in the Battalion. To their left was the right flank of the 47th Division (140 Brigade), with the 1/15th London Regiment (Civil Service Rifles) closest to the 2/7th (Robin Hoods).

That night the battalion worked tirelessly along the whole front digging small lengths of trench, not less than two hundred yards from the road. The ground was frozen to a depth of two feet. There was not one strand of barbed wire. Pack mules brought up stakes, wire and tools and, in limber wagons, supplies of hot food and tea in containers, as well as the odd jar of rum. The Lincolns eventually arrived at daybreak. By 5am the last of the troops had passed through the battalion's lines and at daybreak the Outpost Line troops were left in possession of the whole slope. On the left the 1/15th London Regiment

La Justice Farm, Flesquières, which the Germans had reinforced with concrete and used as a Casualty Clearing Station.

had also been digging and wiring. The engineers had destroyed the dugouts in Bourlon Wood, alerting the enemy to the withdrawal. The Sappers also wanted to do the same thing in the Battalion's sector but Lieutenant Colonel Martyn, knowing what would happen, forbade it.

Before 12 noon the enemy were seen in attack formation coming down the slope of Bourlon Hill. Groups of them halted to look at the derelict tanks but, coming under fire from the British artillery, soon scattered. When they reached the bottom of the hill they were joined by many others who had come down through the wood; they continued to advance but were lost to view because of the valley before Anneux. The German artillery was active throughout the day, registering their guns on the Outpost Line and their old Hindenburg Support Line on which the British were desperately working.

Coming towards the defenders of the Outpost Line were experienced troops from the Eastern Front, the 24th Reserve Division (104th and 107th Reserve Regiments) fielding a force of 6,000 men. Their objectives were the frontage of La Justice, the Outpost Line and then Flesquières itself and the Hindenburg Line System. The first contact with the enemy infantry was made in the early afternoon of the 6th. Firstly, at 2.30pm, a hostile barrage came down on the covering positions; then in the gloom of the winter afternoon the enemy was seen. On the right, five hundred yards east of the village, at the junction of the roads to Cantaing and Marcoing, was the Beet Factory, where 177 Brigade was preparing the Line. A party of Germans attacked the Factory and briefly occupied it, but in a sharp and fierce attack the bayonet men of the 2/4th Lincolns and the 2/5th Leicesters recovered it, taking some prisoners from the 107th Reserve Regiment.

2/7 Sherwood Foresters, Warrant Officers and NCOs.

To their left, between the road to Graincourt and the track going past Orival Wood (about 1,500 yards north of Flesquières), was A Company of the Robin Hoods. The men manning the Outpost Line were not entrenched; all that they had had time to create were shallow holes, forming posts and unconnected to each other. At 3pm the 2/7th Sherwood Foresters came under rifle fire; Lieutenant Hall went out to see what was going on at one of the posts on the extreme right as for the most part the convex land obscured any view of the enemy. He was shot dead. Captain Brewill, the Company Commander, moved up to the post, which was obviously under attack. His men replied to the fire and forced the Germans to fall back. After dark Second Lieutenant Hill, from C Company on the left, took a patrol and reported a large concentration of the enemy in Anneux, about 1,000 yards to the north. At the same time Lieutenant Colonel Martyn, anxious to know the position on the right, sent Lieutenant Ball with another patrol which soon found the Germans very close to the flimsy barbed wire barrier that had been erected in front of La Justice. A short fire fight took place and one of Ball's Platoon Sergeants was lost. At midnight on the extreme left another short battle erupted, but the enemy were driven off. Shouts and moaning were heard: the Battalion's reported

> CSM Clarke with a few men went out and brought in a wounded German who endeavoured to signal to his comrades. Clarke soon persuaded him to stop with the butt end of his revolver.

At midnight the attackers from the 24th Reserve Division had made aggressive contact all along the Outpost Line, thereby indicating that a full scale attack was imminent. Before dawn it was learned that the 6th Division on the right had decided to withdraw from their outpost line due to German pressure. Consequently Major General Romer ordered the men holding right half of his division's Outpost Line to fall back to the right along the track in front of Orival Wood, which ran in to Flesquières. Two machine guns from the Divisional Machine Gun Company were sent up; at first light the enemy were seen to be moving in small groups, encircling the outposts at Flesquières. On the left the 47th (London) Division was now under heavy attack, it was reported that the Germans were in Graincourt and that the enemy were advancing to their rear, up the sunken road behind Flesquières. The OC of the London Brigade on that flank needed help from the Sherwood Foresters but the front was too narrow and another defensive flank on their left impossible. Nevertheless a machine gun was sent to block any advance there. The Germans had now got between the Outpost Line and Flesquières Main Defences; later that day the Outpost Line on the right was evacuated; it was thought that the main attack would come from there. Gradually the Sherwoods and the Lincolns retired over open country into the main lines of defence of Flesquières, the machine guns doing sterling work behind them. When the Division's outpost battalions finally got into Flesquières the Sherwood Foresters found that their casualties were remarkably light.

The Germans had seen enough and subsequently, after the assault had ended and Flesquières was still in British hands, it was found from prisoners that some hundreds of them had died in their attempt on the new line. By the morning of the 7th the British stood on the main line of resistance for the winter. The withdrawal of all the divisions involved had been a remarkable success; an operation in front of an aggressive enemy is always fraught with difficulties. Flesquières would remain in British hands for three months until the great German attack of March 21st.

The casualties of the Battle of Cambrai, including the German counter-attack, came to approximately 47,000 British (of whom 12,000 were taken prisoner, mainly in the opening stages of the German assault) and 50,000 Germans (with a rather smaller proportion of prisoners).

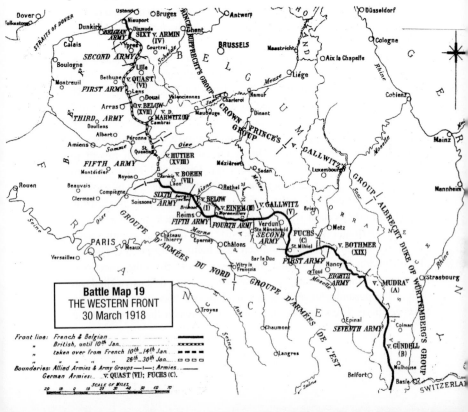

Battle Map 19
THE WESTERN FRONT
30 March 1918

Front line: French & Belgian
"   British, until 10th Jan.
"   taken over from French 10th–14th Jan.
"   26th–30th Jan.
Boundaries: Allied Armies & Army Groups—I—; Armies
German Armies: v. QUAST (VI); FUCHS (C).

Chapter Four

DEFENCE OF FLESQUIÈRES AGAINST THE *KAISERSCHLACHT*, MARCH 1918

The German offensives of spring and summer 1918 have been discussed extensively by historians, most recently, and in an admirable, if controversial book, by Gary Sheffield *Forgotten Victory*. The German High Command, most notably Ludendorff himself made the decision to launch a strike against the Allies in the spring. He wanted to make the best use of the forces liberated from Russia and to end the war before the American military presence became firstly significant, and then overwhelming.

The way to do this, it was felt, was to strike a decisive blow that would force the Allies to come to the peace table on German terms. For all sorts of reasons the planning, both strategic and tactical, and even more so the execution, of this gamble were flawed. Despite great gains, the objectives in every offensive failed. Their failure led the way to the Allied victory of 1918 which was gained to a great extent, without huge scale United States military involvement,

Haig faced a real problem in the early months of 1918. He was deprived by Lloyd George of reinforcement for his divisions (again for controversial reasons beyond the remit of this book) and his weakened forces were also obliged to take over another significant segment of the line from the French. He decided to spread his forces so that the greatest strength was where the strategic danger was greatest – thus the northern sector held by the British Army was strongest and that covering the Somme (Fifth Army) the weakest. To deal with the shortage of manpower, and in line with developing military doctrine, a new defensive scheme was adopted. The well manned front line trenches of

British Prime Minister David Lloyd George

Field Marshal Sir Douglas Haig

115

1915 and 1916 were now a thing of the past. Outpost lines were bolstered by strong points and behind them further strong points, a development of the theory of defence in depth. Some of the Armies adapted to this well, but Fifth Army in particular was so short of men that the doctrine was never fully implemented. This was a contributory factor to the number of the casualties suffered in the offensive.

On top of this the BEF was restructured soon after the New Year. Because Lloyd George would not release reinforcements from the UK (and there were several hundred thousand of these), British divisions were reorganized so that each division would have nine infantry battalions instead of twelve. The process of reorganization had hardly been completed before the Germans struck. The reorganization involved the disbanding of many battalions and amalgamation, as well as the transfer of battalions from one division to another. This did little to help the cohesion of formations, a vital aspect of modern warfare. The impact of this crass, politically imposed decision in view of the imminence of a German offensive has still to be fully explored. Haig had suggested simply reducing the number of divisions, but for various (good) reasons this option was not followed.

It would be Byng's Third Army that would defend the northern part of the Flesquières Salient, including Flesquières village and the ridge. Immediately below was General Sir Hubert Gough's Fifth Army. Gough's sector was forty-two miles long. He had twelve divisions and three Cavalry Divisions and 1,566 guns that would hold and fight the line from Gouzeaucourt south to beyond St Quentin. The 9th (Scottish) Division was at the northern point. Byng's Third Army had fourteen divisions and 1,070 guns on a front of twenty eight miles; V Corps, the most southerly, would fight to hold the 15,000 yards length of the Flesquières Salient.

The 47th (2nd London) Division was below the ridge, about Trescault and Villers-Plouich, a front of 5,000 yards, with its HQ in the chateau at Ytres. At the tip of the salient, a front of 6,000 yards facing north-east, along the eastern edge of Flesquières Ridge, was the 63rd (Royal Naval) Division. It had all three brigades in line, its HQ at Neuville-Bourjonval. The Division had three battalions in the Forward Zone, three, with the Pioneers (14/Worcesters) in the intermediate line and the others in Divisional Reserve at the back of the Battle Zone between Ruyaulcourt and Neuville-Bourjonval. Just north of them, on a 4,000 yards front, was the 17th (Northern) Division, with its HQ two miles behind Havrincourt at Bertincourt. It had two brigades in the line, with four battalions in the Battle Zone; and one brigade, with the

GERMAN PLANS IN PREPARATION FOR 1918.

SCALE OF MILES.

REFERENCE.

Code names MICHAEL; MARS.   Direction
Front attacked on 21st
Place of attacks expected by Supreme War Council
Inter allied Boundaries
Group & Army Boundaries   Armies   SIXTH; FOURTH

Pioneers (7/York and Lancs) behind them and also in the Battle Zone about Hermies.

North of them, and straddling the main Cambrai-Bapaume road, was IV Corps. Its line curved to the north-west, on a 12,000 yard front. On the left, No Man's Land was about 400 yards wide, but in the centre and on the right it was much wider, from half a mile to a mile. This would give the Germans a much longer advance over open ground. On the right, crossing the main road, on a 6,000 yard front, was the 51st (Highland) Division, with its left flank on the prominent Louverval Spur, 3,000 yards along and a 1,000 yards above the main road. Its HQ was at Fremicourt, three miles west of Louverval. All three of its brigades were in the line, each with two battalions divided between the Forward and Battle Zones. The others, with the Pioneers (the 8/Royal Scots) were in reserve towards Beaumetz. On the left of the Division was a great amount of dead ground which made it vulnerable to an attack down the valley. The division's old commander 'Uncle' Harper was now commanding IV Corps, to which his beloved Highlanders belonged. On the Highlanders' left was the 6th Division. It held the line for 6,000 yards across an undulating front, its right facing Bourlon Wood, 9,000 yards away, and its left looking down on Quéant, a mile north-west of Pronville. Beyond this was Third Army's VI Corps, with a 13,000 yards front extending beyond Bullecourt. According to

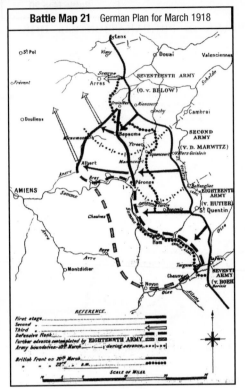

Battle Map 21 German Plan for March 1918

prisoners this was going to be their first objective, a great 'right hook' of fifteen miles north-west of the Salient.

Third Army also had under its command three brigades of field artillery, twenty three batteries of heavy and garrison artillery and twenty siege batteries of super heavies. A defence in depth system had been devised whereby the Forward Zone, approximately of a depth of 3,000 yards, would slow down an initial attack. Behind this was the Battle Zone, 5-6,000 yards deep, where the main battle would be fought. Finally was the Reserve Line, the western edge of which would be 12-15,000 yards from the front line.

The work on the defence lines began in January but for a variety of reasons, chief amongst them being shortage of men and the weather, only the defences of the Forward Zone could be described as adequate by the time the battle commenced on 21 March. Those in the Battle Zone where deep trenches, strong dugouts and many machine gun emplacements were vital were woefully inadequate. The machine gun was the essential item of the defence system. It was assumed the attackers would quickly drive through the narrow Forward Zone, but that they then were to be met in depth by dozens of machine guns and field guns that would even up the disparity in numbers of men. As the advance began to outrun the range of the enemy's guns, the defence in depth would also counter the initial artillery advantage of the Germans.

Of course the defence would need long range visibility to be effective. Before the battle commenced the essential belts of barbed wire had been erected at the Forward Zone but in the Battle Zone, whilst Third Army's was fairly complete, those in the Fifth's were not ready. Furthermore, many trenches were only a foot deep.

V Corps (HQ at Villers-au-Flos) also had two reserve divisions: the 2nd based about Metz, and the 19th (Western) somewhat further back.

The Corps had a particularly difficult task, as it was defending a pronounced Salient, the tip of which was held by the 63rd (Royal Naval) Division.

In the ten days before the attack began the enemy's infantry were quiet. Shortly before the offensive opened the Germans began to shell the salient with poison gas. They first used a mixture of Lachrymatory and Phosgene, but then, they switched to Mustard gas. The 2nd Division was devastated: 99 Brigade was reduced to a 1,000 men and hardly a man had not been affected by it. The division had to be withdrawn and was replaced by the 19th (Western) Division. The 63rd (Royal Naval) Division at Flesquières was similarly hit and suffered almost 3,000 casualties. It could not be relieved from its exposed position and had to stay. Both the 47th and the 17th Divisions also suffered and could not be withdrawn.

Battle Map 22   Extension of the British Front

It was believed that the enemy had hoped the gas bombardment would be sufficient to drive the British out of the salient within the first twenty four hours. It didn't succeed.

Artillery from both sides became very active in the run up to the German attack. Everybody knew it was coming, but not precisely when; men who were due for leave hoped they would get it and not be recalled or return until it was over. [In fact my grandfather, 7/Leicesters, was about to embark on leave when he was recalled just as the attack began. NC.]

The signs of an imminent German assault were first noticed during the evening of the 20th. In addition a thick ground mist began to rise at about 5pm. By 9pm there was indeed a thick fog which continued to get denser as the night wore on. Patrols found No Man's Land empty but at the German wire there were great gaps cut and movements of

119

German troops passing through a communication trench towards the front line.

infantry just behind them. Some prisoners were taken; one who spoke good English told the British that the attack would start at 9.30am on the following morning.

Accordingly some divisions set about manning their battle stations straight away. The British artillery began to shell localities where it was thought that the enemy might be assembling.

Facing V Corps' defenders at Flesquières were the 16th, 21st, 107th, 53rd and the 24th Divisions of General von der Marwitz's Second Army. The 53rd Division had the particular task of protecting the attack on the left flank, pinning down opposing troops until they were turned by the advance further west and were forced to retreat. Then the division was to move on to Havrincourt.

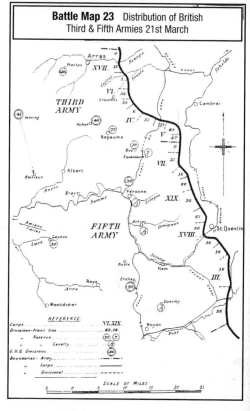

Battle Map 23 Distribution of British Third & Fifth Armies 21st March

At 4.40am the German bombardment started in earnest. After a very heavy trench mortar bombardment obliterated the front trenches occupied by the 63rd (Royal Naval) Division, three attacks were made in succession: at 5.30am, 9.30am and 10.15 am against the right centre, 189 and 190 Brigades of the RN Division, 140 and 141 Brigades of the 47th Division and 50 Brigade of Major General Robertson's 17th Division. The Germans were driven out of the British front line by bombing parties and counter attacks, preventing them from penetrating more deeply or widening the gaps.

All morning the attacks continued. When the fog lifted British machine guns played havoc with the infantry as they advanced in great masses. It soon became apparent to the divisional commanders that as no bombardment had fallen so far on the main road, the enemy soon hoped to make use of it. This suggested that the main assault would fall further north.

By the evening those in the salient's Tip were quite confident, though many men were suffering from the Mustard gas. There were relatively few other casualties whilst the enemy lay in piles in front of the wire and the artillery had been able to maintain its fire all day. As for the Germans, at dusk their fire had greatly reduced.

Further north the assault of General von Below's Seventeenth Army began at 9.45am behind a very heavy bombardment. The German infantry crawled forward under cover of the shelling some twenty minutes earlier. In places they came through the fog and overcame the defenders, few men managing to escaped from the front line to warn those behind them. The Germans came on in six waves of small parties and columns.

The eastern sector of IV Corps was held by 6th and 51st (Highland) Divisions, entrenched across the valleys in front of the old Hindenburg Line. The trenches were on a forward slope and without any deep dugouts; those had that had been dug had generally been demolished by the German bombardments. The communication trenches which led back to Boursies and Louverval at the main road were also constant targets and not defensible. Those stationed there knew that they would

German stromtroopers in attack.

have little chance of escape.

When the Germans gained a footing in the forward trenches of 18 Brigade of the 6th Division held by men from the West Yorks, the DLI and the Essex, they worked eastwards behind the Forward Zone towards 153 Brigade of the Highlanders. The 11/Essex delivered a counter-attack from the communication trenches but could not check the onslaught. Now the Germans began to come on in ten or twelve long lines, split up into small groups, each led by an officer or an NCO with others following in artillery formation. The 51st Division's men occupying the Forward Zone consisted of two and a half companies of the 1/6th and 1/7th Black Watch. The 1/7th Gordon Highlanders, in reserve at Beugny, were now ordered to send up two and a half companies to the Battle Zone. The casualties of the Black Watch were high. Many were killed or buried by the heavy bombardment and the few survivors were so stunned, they were incapable of repelling the invaders. None returned to the Battalion.

By 10am the enemy was closing in from the north. However the resistance on both flanks of the Flesquières salient's Tip had been more than the enemy had bargained for and by the afternoon, apart from

minor local attacks, the assault had stopped. The Germans were tired and had been badly damaged in their first attacks. The British had lost no ground of importance in the salient, but both IV and V Corps north of it had been forced to the rear defences of the Battle Zone, on a ten mile front between the Cambrai-Bapaume road and Croisilles, two miles west of Bullecourt. The losses in the 51st, 6th, 59th and 34th (the latter two defending at Croisilles) Divisions had been very serious.

Where the Highlanders' 152 Brigade had been attacked with flame throwers, the Seaforths and the Gordons had been unable to stop the attack and at a high price in casualties had been forced to withdraw. The 2/York and Lancs of

16 Brigade in the 6th Division had been hit from 4.50am with a heavy barrage and gas at Lagnicourt Trench and the sunken road immediately in the rear and around Battalion Headquarters. At 7.30am the bombardment moved back to the front and reserve line which D and C Companies were occupying. The shelling was intense, lasting for an hour on the front line before lifting for twenty minutes onto the reserve, killing and wounding practically the whole front line company. Only fifteen other ranks out of 150 eventually got back to the reserve line. The German infantry followed and at 8.45am they attacked the left battalion of 18 Brigade, the 1/West Yorks, who lost more than 100 killed. The Germans eventually broke through on that brigade front and the 2/York and Lancs, on the right, were gradually, surrounded, the enemy having penetrated the outskirts of Lagnicourt. A Company was ordered to reinforce the reserve company but had already suffered a large number of casualties from the barrage and could not greatly help. C was under attack from both flanks and also from the right rear and the reserve company was eventually driven out of the reserve lines and withdrew to Dunhelm Avenue. B Company, in Lagnicourt Trench engaged the enemy advancing on them and fought to the finish; the only survivors of the company were a few men who had been left behind in the dugouts. The enemy also nearly cut off Battalion HQ, which was forced to fall back down Dunhelm Avenue with the survivors of the battalion and the 1/Shropshire Light Infantry. At dark on the 21st what remained of the battalion was ordered back to Vaux, two miles south-east of Croisilles, where they spent the night. All that remained of them were 150 men; and only seventy from the Shropshires.

During the early afternoon of the 21st the 25th Division, in reserve at Bapaume, came forward. 74 Brigade was positioned behind the Battle Zone, with the 11/Lancashire Fusiliers and the 9/Loyal North Lancs astride the main road between Beaumetz and Morchies and with the 3/Worcesters in reserve.

Two battalions from 57 Brigade of the 19th Division, the 8/Gloucesters and the 10/Royal Warwicks, along with twelve tanks from Colonel Willoughby's H Battalion, were ordered to recapture Doignies, a thousand yards below Louverval, south of the main road. However it was not before 6.40pm that they moved forward from Velù Wood, 2,000 yards south of the objective. Also it was dark by the time they reached the bottom of the valley and the outskirts of the village, they could proceed no further. The Gloucesters on the right were in a trap and were attacked from Doignies, suffering very badly and

The sad count – a fallen Highlander in Flesquières. Note that his boots have already been 'requisitioned'. A German photograph.

withdrew back up the slope into a trench a thousand yards to the south-west. The battalion would be overwhelmed there on the 23rd. The Worcesters withdrew to the sunken road from Beaumetz but later, all firing stopped. The German attacks against the northern flank of the salient had ceased.

The enemy had certainly gained ground but had not succeeded in breaking through and surrounding the tip of the Flesquières salient. Their time scale was already falling behind. British losses in stemming the massive onslaught here were dreadful: the 47th and 63rd Divisions, lost 600 men killed and 2,500 wounded. In the 2nd London Division and the Naval Division they suffered three thousand gas casualties alone. Those less affected by the Mustard gas could hardly speak and were continually vomiting. The 7/Sherwood Foresters in 178 Brigade of the 59th Division came out of the battle with twelve men: 470 were wounded and many of them were prisoners, including their commander, Lieutenant Colonel Toller. 176 Brigade had also suffered. Lieutenant Colonel H. Johnson, commanding the 5/North Staffordshires, was wounded and with him more than a hundred of his men became prisoner. In 18 Brigade of the 6th Division the 2/DLI had only one officer and ninety four other ranks left. Amongst the officers killed was Second Lieutenant Geoffrey Gates, whose brother had also fallen earlier in the war (March 1917), in an action which won him the VC.

The casualties in the 11/Essex were awful, only two officers out of thirty and 530 other ranks of 639 came away. In 71 Brigade of the 6th Division only about 240 answered the roll call that night from two of its three battalions, the 2/Sherwoods and the 9/Norfolks. The 1/Leicesters had been in reserve for most of the day yet still had only 338 men left: and of the two front line battalions of 16 Brigade, the 1/Shropshire Light Infantry (who had seen their CO Lieutenant Colonel HM Smith captured) and the 2/York and Lancs, only fifty-seven and fifty-four respectively of all ranks returned from the Forward Zone. About 155 guns had been lost that day, along with great amounts of ammunition. The Royal Air Force had also worked hard all day. The 10th Bavarian Regiment of General Otto von Below's Seventeenth Army reported 'about a dozen British low flying battle machines flew up and down and, from an incredibly low height, about twenty metres, bombed our advancing troops'.

As soon as the battle had died down steps were taken to reorganise the line of battle in readiness for the resumption of the attack the next day. In view of the heavy losses in the salient, particularly those from gas in its tip, General Byng decided, with Haig's approval, to order the withdrawal of the front line of V Corps from the apex to the Intermediate Line, four thousand yards to the rear. This withdrawal was not, however, to be made before 1 am on the 22nd.

This line included Highland Ridge in the south, Havrincourt and Hermies, west of Flesquières, beyond the large curve of the dry Canal du Nord. This was an exceptionally strong line, utilising the deep trenches and dugouts of the Hindenburg Line, which had been rewired. Byng was reluctant to leave the land which he had fought for so bitterly five months earlier but it had to be done to avoid what had now become obvious. The Germans clearly hoped to 'pinch out' the salient and capture at least four divisions. The withdrawal of V Corps was completed by 6am on the 22nd without any disruption by the enemy who did not come forward to occupy the Mustard gas infected trenches until 6pm.

IV and VI Corps to the north, after some readjustments following the day's hard fought battles, stood as follows: the 51st Division's 154 Brigade still held the right; 57 Brigade of the 19th Division held the centre, with the 10/Worcesters south-west of Doignies. The Highlanders' 152 Brigade continued the line to the Cambrai-Bapaume road (1/6th Seaforths and one company of the 1/8th Royal Scots

'Casualties were awful.' British dead.

(Pioneers) in line and the 1/4th Seaforths and 1/6th Gordons in reserve); 153 Brigade held the left flank of the division, with all its battalions in the line; behind their left was the 19th Division and the 25th lay in close support.

Two brigades of Royal Garrison Artillery, the 29th and 81st, were sent forward to assist the Highlanders. The 6th Division remained on the right, covering Morchies. The 59th retired to rally round Mory, five miles west of Doignies and situated a mile east of the Bapaume-Arras road, and the 34th Division occupied ground on its left near St Leger. The left flank defence of the salient was in place before dawn.

Although it would be facile to say that it had been a 'good' day for the British defenders, the German operation was in fact already beginning to unravel. Crown Prince Rupprecht had calculated that the British artillery would be swallowed up but this had not been achieved. Ludendorff recorded his disappointment:

> *Crown Prince Rupprecht's Group could not gain ground between Croisilles and Péronne to the extent which had been originally intended, the result was that the enemy in the Flesquières re-entrant was not cut off.*

The Kaiser (who was present at the battle in the south) announced, 'A complete Victory'. And certainly, if success were measured in prisoners and ground gained, that was a reasonable interpretation. It is not really known what German casualties were but they were certainly very high. British prisoners saw masses of German dead being removed, kept together in bundles. They heard from Medical Officers that there were three times the number of wounded that they had expected, and that some felt that the casualties were much too heavy for the offensive to succeed. It is worth noting that the tremendous advances achieved by the British and the Allies in summer and autumn 1918 were also at the cost of huge casualties. Both phases of the war in 1918 cost more on a daily basis than the Somme battle of 1916.

22 March

It was a fine but cold day and the German plan in the sector was still aimed at pinching out the salient. A fog began to form at midnight and continued to obscure the battlefield until mid-morning. The 9th (Scottish) Division, Brigadier General HH Tudor in temporary command, was on the left flank of VII Corps of Fifth Army and on the right of IV Corps' 47th Division on the edge of the salient. The 9th came under attack by the 107th and 54th Reserve Divisions of von der Marwitz's Second Army, moving down through Gouzeaucourt towards Fins, 4,000 yards south of Havrincourt Wood. At 12.15pm Brigadier General Tudor informed Major General Gorringe, 47th Division's commander, that he would probably have to retire that evening, impressing on him the great strength of the attack he was experiencing. He was told that his job was to form a defensive flank if he was forced to retire. Byng, advised of VII Corps' difficulties, arranged that 99 Brigade of the 2nd Division (in reserve), along with a Machine Gun Company, should fill the gap should one appear.

That evening, at 7.30pm, 99 Brigade occupied a position covering Equancourt at Dessart Trench, which ran north-east towards Metz-en-Couture, the vital southern edge of the salient's Battle Zone. Even then the brigade was not in touch with the 47th Division. Things were becoming dangerous on the salient's southern flank of which Byng was aware. There was also considerable pressure on the northern side on IV Corps. It was obvious to him, however reluctant he might be to issue the order, that V Corps would eventually have to withdraw. The decision would depend on the Corps holding on to the large defended areas in the Battle Zone at Metz on the right and Hermies on the left. Even though during the night the 17th and 63rd Divisions had retired for two thousand yards from the very front of the salient's apex, this might not be enough because now the salient was even 'sharper' than before. This was a consequence of the 9th Division's withdrawal to the Battle Zone and IV and VI Corps being driven back to the rear of the front to the north.

Most of Third Army's troops were exhausted, the majority of the battalions were reduced to a company or less, and none had been able to rest during the night. Yet they had to stand in the line as there were no reserves to repel further attacks. At least the garrison in the salient at Flesquières was strong compared to elsewhere, despite the effects of the poison gas. The frontage of the salient now measured only 14,000 yards. This could be drastically reduced by retiring into the Battle Zone and still further by withdrawal behind Havrincourt Wood. The salient would disappear, troops would be freed to join the reserve and there would be less danger of a gap developing between Third and Fifth Armies.

Major General Gorringe

The attack on the 22nd began after a heavy bombardment at 9.30am against Hermies, which was held by the 7/Lincolnshires of 51 Brigade, 17th Division. The assault was made by the three infantry regiments of the 4th Division, the 14th, 49th and the 140th. On that division's right was the 119th Division (both XI Corps), attacking in the same direction. The enemy shelling fell heavily on the village but the defenders were well in front of it and commanding all the open ground the Germans would have to cross. With machine guns and a battery of 79 Brigade RFA firing shrapnel (the infantry helped to bring up more ammunition) the attackers were brought to a halt at 1pm, 450 yards away. They renewed the artillery bombardment but their losses were terrific. The dead lay in piles up against the barbed wire and at 5pm that assault was abandoned. After dark another attempt was made but it also failed.

Meanwhile, to the north of Hermies, a simultaneous attack had been made by the 24th Reserve (Saxon) Division against the 1/4th Gordon Highlanders of 154 Brigade, 51st Division. It broke into their lines at about 1.40pm, making a gap which was immediately filled by the Seaforths and Argylls.

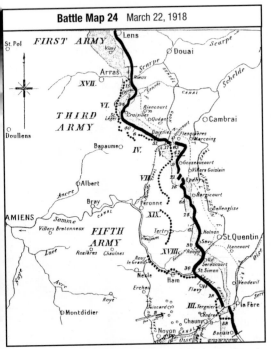

Battle Map 24 March 22, 1918

At 11am the 63rd (Royal Naval) Division was attacked from Marcoing by the 16th Reserve Division and in the afternoon minor efforts were made against the 17th Division between Havrincourt and Hermies. At 5pm they were repeated with flame throwers and at 6.30pm against Havrincourt with much bombing of the 12/Manchesters belonging to 51 Brigade and against the 47th Division's 141 Brigade. The 1/18th London Irish were brought up from Villers-Plouich, the right flank of the salient's tip. The 1/18th were attacked later at about 7.30pm east of Beaucamp but the assault was repulsed. The 53rd Reserve Division met with similar lack of success, came against Havrincourt. At 8pm the German attacks ceased.

The Flesquières salient still held firm. It was now a triangle of 12,000 yards with a base of no more than 8,000 yards. The IV Corps' front from west of Hermies to the Hirondelle Valley, some 12,000 yards, was now held by eight weak brigades of the 51st, 19th, 6th and the 25th Divisions. Behind them were 74, 58, 56 and 7 Brigades. Against this thin line the enemy brought eight divisions: the 119th, 3rd Guards, 39th, 20th, 195th, 1st Guards, 17th and the 111th. Many of them had suffered greatly in the attacks so far.

The attacks on this long northern flank of the salient began at 7am but at 2pm they had made little progress and German casualties were enormous. Soon after, the British troops started to run out of ammunition. The front wavered and shortly there was a six mile gap between Beaumetz and Mory and it seemed as though the Germans would be in Bapaume that night. Fortunately Lieutenant Colonel ED Bryce's B Tank Battalion arrived to give the infantry some close support. However the tanks remained exposed for too long, cruising round, firing at the enemy and without infantry support, except one tank on the right near Morchies which was accompanied by two companies of the 11/Cheshires of 75 Brigade, 25th Division. The little force soon became targets for German artillery on the high ground near Lagnicourt. Sixteen of the tanks were destroyed and only sixty of the Cheshires came out of the action; the solitary tank with them also received a direct hit.

The Germans made no further attacks against 58, 18 and 71 Brigades, but at 5pm the German 24th Reserve Division attacked the 51st (Highland) Division again, near and west of Morchies and there was heavy fighting. Fortunately the German bombardment fell short, thereby driving 200 of their infantry into the British line as prisoners of 153 Brigade. These were German shells from super heavy howitzers falling short on the 3rd Guards Division near Morchies as they were preparing for the assault. The effect was devastating; the survivors streamed back vowing vengeance on the artillery and were only

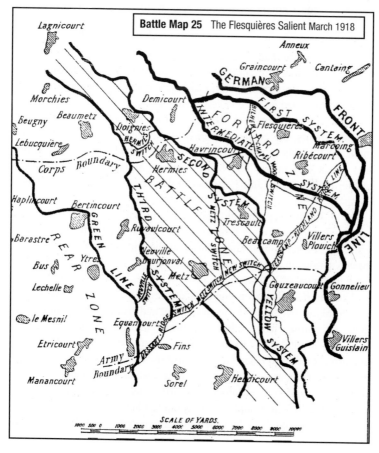

Battle Map 25   The Flesquières Salient March 1918

Captain MA James VC

Captain RF Hayward VC

restrained with difficulty. At about 6pm the 11/Essex facing Morchies were driven back and a number of low flying German aircraft came into the action. The 1/7th Gordons and the 1/6th Black Watch of 153 Brigade, along with a company of the 9/Loyal North Lancs of the 25th Division, formed a shield at the Beaumetz-Morchies Switch trench to help the Essex, thereby barring further immediate advances. They subsequently withdrew to form a defensive flank between the road and Beaumetz. They would hold this line until the end of the day.

57 and 154 Brigades further to the right were attacked at about 6.30pm; two companies of the 1/4th Gordons were overwhelmed and touch with the 17th Division on the right was lost. The 8/Gloucesters in 57 Brigade also had a hard fight. Captain MA James was wounded and taken prisoner, but for his valour that evening he was awarded the Victoria Cross.

There had been other hard battles involving the 25th Division. Captain RF Hayward of the 1/Wiltshire Regiment (7 Brigade) won a Victoria Cross for his valour but he was badly wounded and was taken prisoner.

Thus on the northern flank of the salient, despite terrific bombardments, the enemy had failed to make progress; north of the main road, by sheer weight of numbers, they had advanced a further one and a half miles. The 1/7th Gordons at night time could only muster eight officers and 100 other ranks. They were reorganized as a company.

At 11.30pm Byng was told that the enemy had occupied Fins, which represented a giant finger thrust into the British lines at the junction of Third and Fifth Armies. The security of the garrison in the salient was now in serious question. Shortly after midnight Byng issued orders for the withdrawal of V Corps.

The day had also been one of great aerial activity – of low flying and bombing by the RAF on the battlefield using 25lb bombs from three squadrons. Four other squadrons attacked strategic targets, dropping a total of 730 bombs on enemy reserves and railway junctions. In all thirty-one German aircraft were destroyed and twenty-three driven down, out of control, at a cost of four planes missing, fifteen wrecked and eleven temporarily unserviceable. During the night 805 25lb bombs and six phosphorous bombs were dropped and two dumps set on fire. The Germans retaliated by attacking British aerodromes during the night.

After hearing the official report of the successes so far the Kaiser bestowed on Field Marshal von Hindenburg the Iron Cross with Golden Rays, an honour last bestowed on Blücher in 1814.

23 March

The orders for the execution of the withdrawal were not sent out by the Corps Headquarters until 7.30am, although at 9pm on the previous night the artillery began to pull back. The night was so quiet that withdrawal from the salient was reconsidered and the Sappers were not permitted to do as much destruction as they might have done. British patrols found the Germans lying in scattered groups, exhausted and seemingly not inclined to further activity. The Germans did not stir until after dawn and even British trench mortars and forward 18 pounders were extracted without hindrance.

It was agreed that at 10am the main bodies should begin the withdrawal and that rearguards should remain in position until 1pm. At about 9.30am orders reached battalions that the rearguards should leave the sector Equancourt-Metz-Havrincourt Wood-Hermies at 1pm but that units on the left of this line north of Hermies should remain until 3pm to allow for movement on the right to be completed. Three divisions, from right to left, the 2nd, 47th and the 63rd, would hold the Green Line, which ran north from Equancourt to Ytres-Bertincourt and then curved west to Haplincourt, four miles east of Bapaume. A fourth division, the 17th, which was on the left, would go into reserve two miles beyond the Red Line, prepared if required to spread out there. This Line had not yet been dug.

Until 1pm, the hour of the withdrawal of the rearguards, the Germans made no serious attacks, although they closed up. Away to the left, over the main road, they could be seen moving in force but advancing only slow. They were also coming against the right wing of the Flesquières salient and drove a wedge into the front of the 47th Division near a cemetery, a mile east of Metz-en-Couture. Two of its brigades, 140 and 142, were between the southern edge of Havrincourt Wood and Metz, with 141 Brigade behind at the rear edge of the Battle Zone. The gap between that brigade and 99 Brigade of the 2nd Division, which was reduced to fewer than a 1,000 men, was now visibly widening. This was seen by the Germans who pressed in from the south and south-east against the flank and rear of 140 Brigade. The Londoners fought stoutly, firing more than 25,000 machine gun rounds. Though the enemy, men of the 16th and 21st Reserve

Divisions, managed to capture some trenches but the 47th's line did not break and shortly after midday the enemy gave up as the resistance south of Havrincourt Wood was too strong. Apparently their aim was only intended to hold the divisions at Flesquières until the northern half of a pincer movement could close.

The morning had again been foggy but at 1pm it had cleared and the rearguards, after a short barrage fired to obscure their movements, slipped away to the Green Line. At 3pm, when the 47th Division had assembled about Equancourt, the Germans, who had been following up 99 Brigade, attacked, and the 47th Division's right flank moved forward towards Bertincourt.

At about 5pm the British main bodies had reached the Green Line, but between Flesquières and Havrincourt, the rearguard of 190 Brigade, the 1/Artists Rifles, the 4/Bedford's and the 7/Royal Fusiliers were harassed by the enemy. At Hermies, where the Battle Zone bent backwards, 50 and 51 Brigades of the 17th Division were heavily involved before they could break away. At 1pm, when the advanced parties of the 4th (Pomeranian) Division were attacking behind a heavy barrage, the Germans got into Vélu Wood to the left rear of the 17th Division. Attacking the front of the village, 51 Brigade's position, they almost cut off the 7/Lincolns. The battalion lost half of its small strength of three hundred before it could extricate itself. Although covered on the left by the 10th/Sherwood Foresters, the Lincolns were forced southwards towards the Canal du Nord Working westwards, they eventually reached Bertincourt. The Foresters were also being attacked when D/79th Battery RFA saw their plight and over open sights stopped the Germans and silenced their machine guns. This allowed the Foresters to continue on their way. In their assault on Hermies the Germans almost encircled the 6/Dorsets (50 Brigade), arriving only 250 yards from their line, but they eventually had to withdraw. The

enemy had captured Hermies and now advanced in their old close column formation (this had to be used, arguably, to ensure speed of movement) on the road to Bertincourt. They were met by a motor machine gun battery and divisional machine gunners who exacted a grim revenge. Hundreds were left dead and wounded in the road.

By the evening the Havrincourt-Flesquières Ridge and Havrincourt Wood, the battleground of four months ago, had been vacated. The four divisions which had garrisoned the apex, the tip of the Flesquières Salient in and about the village of Flesquières, had slipped away; but their part in the continuing battle was by no means over. They would continue the fight for three more days until the Germans were back again in the Somme Region.

The retention and what some saw as the over-garrisoning of the Flesquières salient for longer than many had thought right was paid for in more ways than one. Critics of Byng's strategy would argue that if he had withdrawn before the German attack on the 21st, for he knew it was imminent, then tens of thousands of lives would have been spared. A line, held perhaps six miles to the west, might have stopped Ludendorff's advance before it had reached Péronne and Bapaume.

Crossing a section of the Hindenburg Line during the German advance. A very clear idea of the depth and construction of the trench line is evident.

There again, it might not, and the failure of the attack to gain its objectives on Third Army's front was a significant contributory factor to the strategic failure offensive of 21 March.

Casualties in the salient were very high. On the first day at Flesquières, Third Army had lost 14,000 men, of which 3,100 were known to be killed. Sadly, of that total, only 400 can be found in the cemeteries in the vicinity. This is reflected in the headstones in the cemeteries indicating an unknown soldier, and on the walls of the missing at Pozières and Arras. The memorial at Pozières lists 12,751 names of men from the Fifth Army and at Arras there is a similar number from the Third Army amongst the 35,000 names commemorating the missing of all the battlefields about Arras. The total casualties in both Armies for the seventeen days of fighting until the offensive finally came to a halt were 160,000; 75,000 of them were prisoners. Approximately half of the casualties came from Third Army, of which some 40,000 came from the Flesquières salient: approximately 10,000 killed, 15,000 wounded and 15,000 prisoners. The Germans estimated that on the first day they had lost, on the whole front, 11,000 killed and 29,000 wounded; hardly any were lost as prisoners – perhaps 300. Such casualties were not simply the result of military incompetence (though doubtless this was a contributory factor) but rather to the fact that the fighting was between two well balanced, well trained and well equipped forces.

Chapter Five

THE LAST BATTLE: SEPTEMBER 1918

The German offensives in the spring and summer of 1918 were strategic failures. The ground gained was, however, impressive – the more so because of the high cost in casualties that the Allies had originally suffered to gain it. From Britain came tens of thousands of trained but inexperienced men; the majority were young men of barely eighteen. The BEF became known as 'The Boys' Army'.

Haig was convinced that victory could be achieved in 1918, and by the summer all his Armies had the logistical capability to sieze the initiative. Not least would be the contribution of Byng's Third Army. His Army now consisted of four Corps: IV Corps commanded by Lieutenant General 'Uncle Harper' (of the 51st (Highland) Division fame), it consisted of the 5th, 37th, 42nd and the New Zealand Divisions; V Corps, commanded by Lieutenant General CD Shute, comprised the 17th, 21st, 33rd and 38th Divisions; VI Corps, commanded by Lieutenant General Sir Aylmer Haldane, had the Guards, 2nd, 3rd, and 62nd Divisions; XVII Corps, commanded by Lieutenant General Sir Charles Fergusson, had the 52nd, 57th and 63rd Divisions. There would be some transfers of divisions within Third Army before the attack on the Hindenburg Line took place on 25 August. However it would be IV and VI Corps that were to be involved in the final capture of Flesquières Ridge, on the 26th/27th of September 1918. The formations which achieved the capture were the Guards, 3rd, 42nd and 62nd Divisions.

After intensive training and various battles by Fourth Army, the British had forced back the great German salient on the Somme. Byng on 20 August issued to his army the following Battle Instruction:

The Third Army has been ordered to press the enemy back towards Bapaume without delay and to make every effort to prevent the enemy from destroying road and rail communications.

Third Army was to join in the great Allied offensives which, in only thirteen weeks, would see victory. Within a week, elements of IV and VI Corps had reached the Arras-Bapaume-Péronne road and moved beyond Bapaume into land devastated by the German army's withdrawal to the Hindenburg Line in the spring of 1917. Battles for these villages began once more, particularly for the 42nd (East

Lancashire) Division, now on the left flank of IV Corps. Its longer serving soldiers retained bitter memories of the fighting for Riencourt, Villers au Flos, Ytres and Neuville-Bourjonval in the original German retreat to the Hindenburg Line in the spring of 1917. Now they were called upon to repeat the process.

The fighting was bitter. Ludendorff had ordered that the Hindenburg Line was the furthest line eastwards to which he could contemplate a withdrawal; casualties on both sides mounted. On 3 September, Third Army issued an order for its right wing, IV, V and VI Corps, to maintain the pressure on the Germans. VI Corps was to capture Lagnicourt, only seven miles west of the Canal du Nord, without delay. The canal was not all dry. The tunnel from Ytres to Ruyaulcourt was filled with water held in by a dam at the Ruyaulcourt end but from there, north, beyond Moeuvres and the Third Army area, it was empty.

Captured German 5.9 inch gun near Cambrai.

The divisions of IV, V, and VI Corps had been leap-frogging since the start, and by 5 September IV Corps had crossed the canal and was close to Havrincourt Wood. The Hindenburg Line here, coming from the east, ran across the north-eastern tip of the wood then turned sharply to the north, using and following the canal. VI Corps, on the right, also advanced on the same day: the Guards Division attacked the Spoil Heap on the canal's west bank, north-east of Hermies, but failed to take all their objectives. On the 6th the New Zealand Division of IV Corps took Metz-en-Couture and the southern part of Havrincourt Wood. The army was closing in on Flesquières Ridge. It was the strongest section of the Cambrai defence line, securing the gateway to the city and the enemy were determined to hold on to it. Byng brought the 63rd (Royal Naval) Division forward as a reserve behind VI Corps. It had been the last formation out of Flesquières in March 1918.

For the next three days there was only patrol action and no change in the situation; but the weather had also turned very wet. The Germans had potentially six lines of defence and the opposition to both Third

and Fourth Armies was still formidable. Byng said it was essential to attack quickly, arguing every day without battle made the enemy that much stronger. He pointed out that the condition of the German troops was poor; and that many would surrender if they dared – but persistent and constant attack was vital. Indeed it was true (though Byng did not know this). Ludendorff was severely rattled by the success of the Allies.

On 12 September the battle for Havrincourt began. 'The 62nd Division will recapture Havrincourt Village', ordered Major General Sir Robert Wigham, the division's new commander.

Sergeant Leonard Calvert VC.

Attacking from the south-west through Havrincourt Wood at dawn on 12 September, 186 Brigade (Duke of Wellington's), the 2/4th leading, went forward northwards and then turned to the east, with its left flank at the southern edge of the village. By 7.30am they had captured the Hindenburg front system and when the British heavy artillery lifted off the village the chateau was taken. After hard fighting, the brigade was established at 11.30am on the eastern edge of the village.

187 Brigade sent forward the 2/5th and part of the 2/4th KOYLIs with the 2/4th York and Lancs, but they were strongly opposed by the enemy, particularly from a strong point 450 yards south of the village, one of their old fortified mine craters which had given trouble in November 1917. Sergeant Leonard Calvert of the 2/5th KOYLIs rushed forward alone, capturing two machine guns and killing the crew. He was awarded the Victoria Cross. The attack now went well but the brigade could not make contact with 186 Brigade until nightfall because of the murderous fire sweeping the open ground.

At 6.30pm the Germans made a determined effort to recapture Havrincourt. Part of a fresh German division, the 20th in support of the 52nd Reserve Division, attacked, accompanied by low flying aircraft and under cover of a violent bombardment. The German onslaught fell mainly on the 2/4th Hampshires of 186 Brigade and the 2/5th KOYLIs of 187 Brigade, but it was eventually repulsed by machine gun and rifle fire aided by artillery.

Therefore, the 62nd (West Riding) Division held Havrincourt and the Hindenburg Front System. The general advance of the Third Army had averaged a mile on its five mile front. It would soon be Flesquières' turn. Only the 62nd Division of VI Corps had so far crossed the canal, west of Havrincourt Wood, the remainder was at and about Hermies, north of the great eastward bend of the canal and west of the almost straight stretch running north, part of the main Hindenburg defence lines. This area was covered by the 3rd and the Guards Divisions. On 20 September orders for Third Army to proceed with its offensive were issued. Facing it was the right of the German Second Army and the left of their Seventeenth, the junction being near Havrincourt. From north to south there were at least thirteen and a half of their divisions against fourteen British. VI Corps was to capture Flesquières Ridge, the village (now a total ruin and on fire) and the spur running northwards to Graincourt. Then it was to clear the Hindenburg Support Line running across the front of Flesquières and down the valley side to Ribécourt. IV Corps was to capture Beaucamp on the southern ridge of the bowl and Highland Ridge at the far, eastern, side of it and Villers-Plouich. Brigadier General Baker-Carr, commander of 1st Tank Brigade, allotted twenty-four tanks to IV Corps and the same number to the VIth. The IIIrd Brigade RAF, with fifteen Squadrons, with a total of 261 aircraft, would cooperate with Third Army.

During the night of the 26th/27th, in spite of low clouds and rain, the bombers attacked selected German Headquarter targets. To ensure all was in place for the assault the attack was scheduled to commence on Third Army's front on 27 September; Zero Hour for IV and VI Corps would be 5.20am and would be preceded by a short, intense, artillery bombardment. The divisions of IV Corps would be south of Flesquières Ridge. 42nd (East Lancashire) Division was on the left flank, attacking Trescault. 127 Brigade, the Manchesters, would come out of Femy Wood, 125 Brigade, the Lancashire Fusiliers, on the right flank just below Beaucamp 126 Brigade would follow through. It was familiar ground for the Lancastrians who had been here in the spring of 1917. The 5th Division would take and clear Beaucamp. The 42nd Division's attack would start three hours after Zero to allow the flanking divisions to take the heights on both sides of the valley. In the event Beaucamp proved a difficult nut to crack and would not fall easily. The defences' machine guns cut swathes in the Lancashire Fusiliers on the right and the Manchesters on the left as they came out of the Grand Ravine heading for Ribécourt and Highland Ridge. It was evening before they had fought across the valley and the Manchesters had linked up with the 62nd Division at Ribécourt. The Hindenburg Main Line south of Flesquières Ridge had been smashed, this time almost without tanks. Eight had been allotted to the two brigades, six of which had failed for one reason or another; but two had proved of valuable assistance in dealing with machine gun emplacements.

**Captain
C.H. Frisby VC.**

**Lance Corporal
T.N. Jackson VC.**

**Lieutenant
Colonel Lord
Gort VC.**

VI Corps had a long way to go before they could get to grips with its main objective, Flesquières. Its first objective was the Canal du Nord and then the Hindenburg Main Line. Its second was the Hindenburg Support Line on the southern and western edges of the village. The third was the eastern end of the village, the road to Cantaing, the formidable defensive structure of the Sugar Factory and then Ribécourt. From there it would advance towards Marcoing and Premy Chapel. The first advance was of 1,500 yards. The Guards Division on the left and the 3rd Division on the right would have twelve tanks each.

The Guards' engineers and pioneers had constructed ramps and trestle bridges over the canal and in fact were still constructing them as the battle opened. The bottom of which was filled with barbed wire barricades. 2 Guards Brigade, (Coldstream and Scots Guards) went forward at 5.20am but the Coldstream were held up by the wire and a machine gun emplacement built under the ruins of the demolished bridge of the Graincourt-Demicourt road. Attacked by Captain CH Frisby and four men, one of whom was Lance Corporal TN Jackson, the enemy position which had seriously delayed the Coldstream advance was overcome. Both Frisby and Jackson were awarded the Victoria Cross but Jackson was killed later on in the day.

This delay meant that the Coldstream fell behind the barrage. Heavy fire struck them and brought their advance to a halt two hundred yards short of the Hindenburg Support Line. They stayed there until 2.40pm, protecting the brigade's left flank. The Scots Guards had achieved their first objective by 7am.

1 (Guards) Brigade, Brigadier General C de Crespigny, had followed to the right of the 2nd with some success until 11am. When they were abreast of the village, strong enemy fire came from the Sugarbeet factory – which had been turned into a fortress – on the Cantaing road and they were held up.

3 (Guards) Brigade, the Grenadiers and Welsh, had lost its commander, Brigadier General G Follet, killed earlier that morning, and Lieutenant Colonel Lord Gort took command. He would be twice wounded that day and be awarded the Victoria Cross for his conspicuous gallantry. (In due course he became the commander of the B.E.F in its campaign in northern France in 1940.) The brigade was

142

due to pass through the second objective at 9.50am but was forced to wait.

The 2nd Division had arrived close behind the Guards at the Canal du Nord and had crossed it behind 3 (Guards) Brigade. At 2pm it had closed up north of Flesquières at Orival Wood.

On the right of the Guards Division was Major General CJ.Deverell's 3rd Division. During the previous day its engineers had been busy, despite enfilading fire, building a trestle bridge on the left of the cutting, strong enough to take medium artillery across the hundred feet deep cutting of the canal. Two companies, consisting of about twenty-four tanks, had been allotted to the division. They would advance in support of 8 Brigade, consisting of Royal Scots, Royal Scots Fusiliers and King's Shropshire Light Infantry and 76th Brigade's Gordon Highlanders, Suffolks, King's Own, and attack Flesquières directly. 9 Brigade, Northumberland Fusiliers, Royal Fusiliers, Kings Liverpools would be on the right on the edge of the Ridge. It was these troops the that 42nd Division could see and for whom they were waiting. The Scots and the Shropshires advanced at 5.20am to meet fierce opposition from the enemy positions on the railway embankment but, with the help of six tanks, by 6.45am had reached the Hindenburg Support Line on the western edge of Flesquières. On the right the Northumberlands, Royal Fusiliers and King's Liverpools had fought along the southern edge of Flesquières. The Royal Fusiliers reached the blazing ruins of Ribécourt, set on fire by RAF bombers, but it was not until 11.30am, assisted by the 2/4th KOYLIs of the 62nd Division (that division having come through after the 3rd), that Ribécourt was taken.

76 Brigade would pass through 8 Brigade at 7.10am. To quote from the Regimental History of the Gordon Highlanders:

On the 26th they had rested from 2pm to 5pm and in the evening marched to the assembly trenches. The night was quiet and the enemy suspected nothing. At 5.20am on the 27th the quietness was shattered by the tremendous fire from our artillery. At 5.45am the 8th Kings Own and the 1st Gordon Highlanders advanced, at this stage of the war the battalion was filled with young soldiers and inexperienced platoon commanders. Despite some confusion the wire was overcome and quickly they were in a fight with determined defenders, suffering considerable losses. Nevertheless they pressed forward following the new barrage to the second objective. The ground was covered with a maze of old fortified shell craters and trenches. Some of the German machine

143

gunners kept up their fire until rushed at close quarters and showered with grenades. The Hindenburg Trench skirting Flesquières did not prove particularly difficult but in the southern part of the ruins the confusion became great and Captain CH Lees scraping together sixty men burst into the northern part, clearing it and came out on the northern side into the Irish Guards position. He was awarded the DSO.

There the advance through Flesquières was halted in face of fire from the Sugar Factory and German 77mm field guns firing over open sights. The 3rd Division had almost taken Flesquières and was now halted, 76 Brigade alone had taken 614 casualties, 500 of them wounded. The 62nd Division had begun to come forward from its positions at Havrincourt to pass through the 3rd, sheltered by the original barrage and later, at 9.20am, by some artillery batteries that had come forward. By 7.15am 185 Brigade had crossed the canal and with 187 Brigade went forward; 185 Brigade was ahead and, following 76 Brigade, took the northern part of the village by 9.50am. At this hour the Sugar Factory fortress was still holding everybody up and 185 Brigade suffered serious casualties. About midday the Germans put in a counter-attack from Premy Chapel Hill, forcing the Guards and the West Yorkshires back into the trenches about Orival Wood. Later the Sugar Factory was overcome; 187 Brigade had linked up with 9 Brigade of the 3rd Division and 127 Brigade of the 42nd (East Lancashire) Division in Ribécourt and the last battle for Flesquières was ended.

The casualties had been heavy but the way was open for the capture of Cambrai. In fact the town was evacuated on the night of 8/9 October and by 5am on the 9th on most of the front of Third Army little was left of the Germans except weak rearguards. The German Regimental Histories gave a doleful account of the fighting at Flesquières, one noting: 'The troops were completely used up and burnt to cinders'.

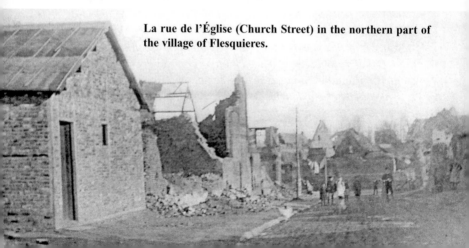

La rue de l'Église (Church Street) in the northern part of the village of Flesquieres.

TOUR ONE

The tour covers the arrival of the tanks and the 62nd (West Riding) Division to the battle area at Havrincourt Wood and its successful attack on the western end of the Flesquières Ridge and north to Graincourt.

Battle Maps: 4,5, 7, 8, 9, 10, 11, 12.   Tour circuit distance: Approx **15 miles**.

Assuming that you have stayed at Cambrai, drive down the N30 for about 11 miles, proceeding through Fontaine-Notre-Dame. *Please note that there are numerous 'priorities from the right' in Fontaine, even from the most minor of roads. Suitable caution (and speed) MUST be adopte*d. Passing Bourlon Wood on the right until, about two miles further on, you will see a turning to your left, the D18E to Beaumetz-les-Cambrai; take it. You will be coming this way again, visiting some of the places you are now passing, on subsequent tours, for this is the edge of the 'arc' west of Flesquières.

You go past the village of Lebucquière on your right and skirting Vélu Wood on the left, within a mile you arrive at a minor road junction on the northern edge of Bertincourt. Turn left round the edge of the village, following the minor road round to the north-east corner, and Chateau Cemetery **(1)**.

The village was prominent in the battles of 1917 and 1918. It was also the base of a German Air Force Fighter Squadron in 1916 and later in the war the Red Baron, Manfred von Richtofen, flew from here. There were a number of airfields in the surrounding villages.

The British fought here twice and the 47 graves (with only two 'unknown') tells the tale, graves mainly from the 37th Division, the 7th KOYLIs, in March 1917 as they pursued the Germans back to the Hindenburg Line and, doing the same thing a year and a half later, the 42nd (East Lancashire) Division in 1918. My father, from Burnley, served with the latter in this area twice. A then prominent cotton manufacturer from the town owner has a son buried in row B Grave 16, Second Lieutenant JE Kippax, aged 20, killed on 20 September 1918. The 1/7th Lancashire Fusiliers lost Major RH Cade, aged 27, on the 27th of the same month. Though the cemetery is small it has a lot of memories for Lancashire men.

The tour follows the D7, going left out of the village to Ruyaulcourt. Before doing so note a track from the cemetery leading to **(2)** and down there, about a mile away, is where 'G' Battalion of the Tank Corps unloaded from the train bringing them forward for the battle on 20 November 1917. However, turn left, following the curving road to the right and within a short distance is the line of the old railway track running down to **(2)**. Just before you enter Ruyaulcourt there is a CWGC sign indicating Ruyaulcourt Military Cemetery **(3)** to the left, along a narrow sunken track after about 500 yards along it. It is better to leave your car at the beginning of this track and the walk is well worth it. This sunken lane was the location of some of the British artillery in both 1917 and 1918. The cemetery holds 348 graves, with only 10 unknown. There are 86 men from the 42nd (East Lancashire) Division, mainly from the spring of 1917, casualties from forcing the Germans back to the Siegried Stellung. In row F Grave 8, over on the left hand side, is Lieutenant Colonel TAD Best DSO, killed when commanding the 2/5th Duke of Wellington's going through Havrincourt. Next to him, killed at the same time, is Lieutenant JG Bodker. Close

145

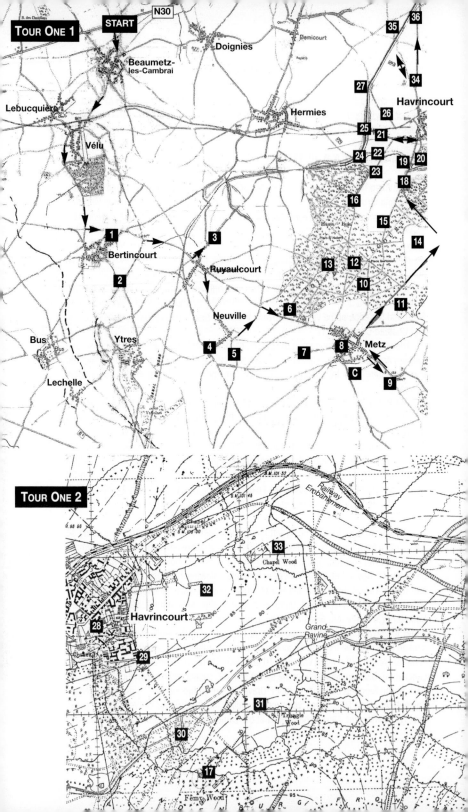

to him, in Grave 15, is Lieutenant The Hon. AM Kinnaird MC, who was mortally wounded on 26 November 1917 at Fontaine-Notre-Dame but rescued by Sergeant John McAuley of the Scots Guards who was awarded the Victoria Cross for this action. There is a friend of my father in row E Grave 11, Driver Albert Gregory of B/210(Burnley) Battery, killed on 14 July 1917 and there are others from the same Territorial Artillery Brigade who had also served on Gallipoli in 1915. There is a 19 year old machine gunner in row N Grave 7, Jack Turnbull, killed on 27 September 1918, whose parents named their home, on Kilmarnock Road, Glasgow, 'Ruyaulcourt', in his memory.

Drive into the village, turn left at the crossroads and then take the right fork for Neuville-Bourjonval **(4)**. It was here that Major General Braithwaite, commanding the 62nd (West Riding) Division, had his headquarters and whence the division set out for battle. In the village head south for Neuville-Bourjonval Military Cemetery**(5)**. It is on the right, 100 yards down a muddy track. Originally, at the communal cemetery, there was a large German cemetery (528 men) but the bodies were all removed after the war. The British cemetery holds 198 graves (nine unknown). 48 are of the 42nd (East Lancashire) Division from their time at the Hindenburg Line and Trescault in the spring of 1917. Many others are of men from the Rifle Brigade, killed during the same period, in fact the ridge immediately east of here was called Green Jacket Ridge. Of course there are men here killed in the Cambrai battle and the holding of the Flesquières Salient. In row E Grave 28 is Lieutenant Colonel Herbert St Hill, aged 52, of the Royal North Devon Hussars in which he served for eighteen years. He had fought in the Matabele, Angoni, South Africa and Gallipoli campaigns, where he had commanded the 6th Lincolns.

Retrace your route to the village, turn right and right again onto the D7 and at **(6)** is the corner of Havrincourt Wood where G Battalion of the Tank Corps gathered for the attack, leading the 62nd Division into it. They moved towards the front line in the north, the battle maps indicating the layout then. The tanks went up the left hand side of the wood to enter the attack line 2,000 yards away. It is possible to walk in the wood but note that the wood is private property. Nearby and almost opposite the wood's corner, on the right hand side of the road **(7)**, was the HQ of 153 Brigade Royal Field Artillery. Some of its men are buried in the cemeteries already visited. We will be coming along this road on later tours.

Metz-en-Couture was a ruin in the autumn of 1917. The village has a system of ancient underground caverns and tunnels – as most of them do in this area (the stone was extracted for building purposes) – which were used by both armies in the war. Below the village **(C)** was the cavalry concentration area. At the crossroads **(8)** was a huge mine crater blown by the Germans. In fact almost all the crossroads in this area had been similarly dealt with. Metz-en-Couture Communial Cemetery British Extension **(9)** is alongside the communal one. In plot II, at the end of row E, Grave 24, lies Captain George Henry Tatham Paton VC, MC, aged 22, of the 4th Grenadier Guards. He was killed on 1 December 1917 at Gonnelieu, four miles

Captain George Henry
Tatham Paton VC, MC

147

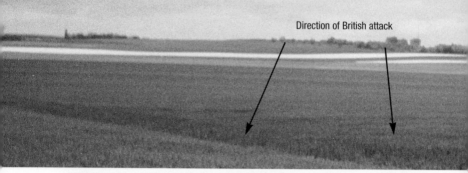

Direction of British attack

Looking over the great depth of the Hindenburg trenches and barbed wire from the German point of view. The Spoil Heap can be seen in the distance and the Canal du Nord is this side of it. The direction of the British attack was towards the camera.

due east, just beyond Gouzeaucourt, trying to stop the enemy in its great counter-attack of 30 November. His men's bravery helped to form what would become the Flesquières salient. Many of the 474 graves (44 unknown) are from the battles of 21 March 1918. Amongst others you will find three lieutenant commanders of the 63rd (Royal Naval) Division close together in plot II row F, all killed at the same time. Lieutenant Commander AU Campbell MC lies in Grave 5. From the 47th Division's battle about Metz on 23 March 1918, trying to hold the southern flank of the Flesquières salient, there are many men here from its London Regiment battalions, their graves scattered amongst the rows. The RSM of the 24/Londons, Mr HW Norris DCM, is remembered on a Special Memorial. Private WJ Austin aged 26 of the same regiment you will find in plot IV row B Grave 3. In plot II row C Grave 3 is Major R.O.C. Ward of D Battalion the Tank Corps, killed on 20 November at Flesquières, his tanks leading the Highlanders. There are also some German graves.

Return to the crossroads **(8)** and turn right on the D17, recalling that this ruined village was packed with Highlanders on 19 November 1917, and soon you enter the south-east corner of Havrincourt Wood. Pause for a moment and look around. On the right of the road **(11)** was where D Battalion of the Tank Corps was parked up on the night of 19 of November; Major Ward would have been there – how close is his grave from where he went into battle. On the other side of the road **(10)** was E Battalion. Just as the road leaves the wood, stop and look at **(12)** and **(13)**. **(12)** was Hubert Road which runs across the wood in a north-westerly direction. Along it were rows of guns for the unregistered barrage of 20 November. Around **(13)** was Brigadier General RB Bradford VC's 186 Brigade (Duke of Wellington's) waiting to go forward into the attack on Havrincourt at 9am on the 20th. The whole West Yorkshire Division was deep in the wood. This is the Trescault Road; **(14)** was known as Trescault Valley. About a 1,000 yards to your left, in the right hand side of the wood **(15)**, was 185 Brigade (West Yorks). Look at the battle map for a description of the tracks in the wood.

Major Ward.

Take the left fork onto the D15 just in front of Trescault; the road drops down into Havrincourt Wood and we are now going through the great depth of barbed wire and deep trenches of the Hindenburg Line which would have filled our view to the right and which ran north along the line of this modern road. It then ran round the south of Havrincourt village to cross the road at **(18)** and continued north along, and then crossed, the Canal Du Nord. At **(17)** the West Yorks of 186 Brigade, led by the tanks smashing down

Spoil Heap Canal du Nord

the wire, went into Femy Wood, where many of the trees had been cut down by the Germans to give them a better field of fire, the tree stumps providing a great hazard for the tanks. The wood will be examined later. At **(18)** was the fortified mine crater Boggart Hole; and just beyond it **(19)** was another one, Snowden. **(20)** is Chateau Wood. Proceed very slowly and on the right, by the road edge on a low bank, you will see, almost hidden by the undergrowth, a large concrete machine gun bunker into which – and at your own risk – you can enter.

The first road junction on the left (still in the Hindenburg Line) is the D5 to Hermies; take it and stop at **(21)**, a junction with a track running down the open valley (Oxford Valley) into the wood. This is the site of the Vesuvius mine crater, taken by the KOYLIs at bayonet point on the 20th. Just behind is a large water tower; it was from here that the front of the Hindenburg Line, coming up out of Femy Wood, ran north, making full use of the dry Canal du Nord. It was through there that 187 Brigade advanced towards Graincourt. Consider several thousand infantry, KOYLIs and York and Lancs, led by the best part of thirty tanks, and with a bombardment falling all about. What a sight for the brave German infantry manning their line, doubtless terrified at what they could see. Drive down the track to the small stand of trees and farm buildings, and then turn around. Here was **(22)**, the Etna mine crater and Dean Copse, both taken by the Yorkshiremen that morning. The roads and tracks in the wood have mostly Lancashire names; for example, Dean Copse is named after a street in Manchester. It was here that the 42nd (East Lancashire) Division faced the Hindenburg Line in the spring of 1917. As you drive back up the hill you are behind the tanks and in the footsteps of the Yorkshire men of 187 Brigade, advancing with bayonets fixed under heavy fire from the machine guns and artillery.

At the top turn left and, after you have crossed the bridge over the autoroute, stop and park before the old railway and road bridge **(25)** at the gorge. The view here is marvellous. Remember that the great 'ditch' was empty. See the view the enemy had over Havrincourt Wood and all the land over which the British had to advance. Wigan Copse has gone now, under the new road. Look north to **(27)** the Spoil Heap, now a tree covered hill, a fortified prominence of the Hindenburg Line taken that morning by the Irishmen of 109 Brigade of the 36th (Ulster) Division, advancing alone up the west side of the 'Ditch'.

Return now to the main road, turn left and go into the village and at the village green look at the magnificent gates of the chateau. Destroyed in two world wars and twice rebuilt, it is now empty. The Germans used it as an Headquarters and the Kaiser stayed there. On 20 November 1917 it was fortified and presented a significant problem for the 62nd Division. It was here as the 186 Brigade advanced through the village, thinking it

German bunker by the roadside as you approach Havrincourt from Trescault. It was used against the attack of 186 Brigade.

was totally subdued, that Lieutenant Colonel Best, commanding 2/5th Dukes was shot dead. At the green, which was then a water filled crater, Second Lieutenant FW McElroy got his tank, G3, stuck; but he continued to fight it, though his crew were dead or wounded. It would be a good idea to re-read now the story of the battle here before moving on, to get a full 'picture' of it all. The house on the corner is actually a very welcoming pub and the charming lady will be pleased to see you. Many men, of both sides, fought bravely and died in this village. The sign for the Grand Ravine Cemetery, fixed to a wall at the corner, directs you to the rear of Chateau Farm; from these buildings was the gunfire which killed Colonel Best. At **(29)** is the tall, granite column war memorial to the 62nd (West Riding) Division, often missed. This is the battleground of the West Yorkshires and 186 Brigade, the Dukes. Fifty yards further along there is a narrow track, usually passable, going down to the right. Take it and, as it drops down, remember that tanks of 'G' Battalion came up here, the barbed wire heavy and thick, interlaced with deep trenches. At the bottom follow the track through the trees and then you are in a clearing at the western end of the Grand Ravine with **(30)** its cemetery in the middle of the clearing. I always think this a particularly sombre place, particularly on a dull winter afternoon. What a terrific scene it was on 20 November 1917, filled with tanks and fighting men. Before entering the cemetery, look around. It was here in September 1918 that the Manchesters of the 42nd East Lancs Division went up the hill, along the track opposite the one you came down, fighting through the rebuilt Hindenburg Line and going on towards final victory. Behind you, along the valley, is Ribécourt.

There are 139 graves (eleven unknown) in the cemetery. The original graves, row B, were made by the Divisional Burial officer in December 1917, where you will find men from the November battle. The same officer completed the other two rows in October 1918 when the 62nd Division was here again. I was surprised to find, when I first came here thirty years ago, one of my namesakes at the far end of row C, Private HH Horsfall, who was fighting with 2/20th London Regiment in September 1918. His family in Todmorden, near Burnley, were delighted to receive a photo of his grave and to resume contact with another member of the clan. There are many young men, such as in row B grave 6, Lance Corporal Ernest Atkinson from Leeds aged 19 killed on 20 November as the West Yorks stormed through the Hindenburg Line or a reinforcement to the Dukes, Private Thomas Hailwood (row A Grave 15), aged only 18 and killed on 28 September 1918. Near him in Grave 33 is Private Fred Petty MM aged 19 of the KOYLIs, from Hull and also killed in September 1918.

At **(31)** is Triangle Wood, you can still find traces of trenches beneath the bracken; and ahead up the open slope on the left was T Wood **(32)**, attacked by the West Yorks as was Chapel Wood **(33)**, in the Hindenburg Support Line. They fought up the valley side towards the Flesquières-Havrincourt track and the Blue Line. If there is time it is an interesting walk up there.

Go back up the track into the village and take the D15 northwards, traversing the autoroute and at the 'V' junction close to its northern side stop and visit Lowrie Cemetery **(34)**, below the road in the fork. Go down the track towards the canal and **(35)**. The track is somewhat bumpy, cutting through the Hindenburg Line which filled this land, running northwards. 187 Brigade, the KOYLIs and York and Lancs, stopped about here on the Brown Line and then 186 Brigade came through, going for Graincourt. At the end of the track is the Canal Du Nord. Lock 7 is about 500 yards away. It was here in the dry basin of the lock that Bradford had his Brigade HQ in the days just before the great German counter-attack of 30 November 1917. He was mortally wounded there by a shel and you will see his grave at Hermies on Tour 4.

Return to **(34)**. This small cemetery was made by the Burial officer, Captain Lowrie, of the 3rd Division in the advance and battle for the Flesquières Ridge (Tour 5) in September/October 1918. It holds 251 men (46 unknown). It is a bit difficult to get to. The men buried here might well have realised that the war was almost won and many of them, survivors of four years, must have hoped they would see home again. In E 19 there is an 'old man', Private Stephen Adams aged 41 from Bute, of the 2/Royal Scots. Had he fought with his battalion since 1914 when it saw action at Mons? Look along row J, in Grave 10 is the 20 year old Lieutenant Roland Bedford of the Devons, the holder of the MC and Bar,

Bridge over Canal du Nord. Attacked by Guards Division in September 1918. There are bunkers in the ruins of the bridge.

Two VCs Bridge

Guards attack

who had enlisted in the ranks in July 1915. There are many decorated men buried here: for example in row F Grave 24 lies CSM JK Rollo DCM, MM, Medaille Militaire, aged 26, of the Gordon Highlanders. There is a young American boy in G 13, Private John Alexander Churchill MacLachan, also of the Gordons but who came to enlist from North Carolina.

Turn left on the D15 for Graincourt and within a mile you will see a Cross of Sacrifice on a small hill, 500 yards to the right. Take the track to it (it is usually solid but muddy). Before you enter stop and look out over the canal to the west. This is Sanders Keep **(36)**,

a strong German fortification in the 1918 reinforced Hindenburg Line, attacked by the Guards Division on 27 September 1918. There are 142 graves (seven unknown). Once 49 German graves were here, the keep's defenders, but they are now in Cambrai. Two Victoria Crosses were awarded for bravery in the Guards' assault and one of these men, a Coldstreamer, Lance Corporal Thomas Norman Jackson VC, aged 21, is still here. He had followed Captain CH Frisby across the 'dry ditch', assaulting the machine gun posts and fortifications. The captain was also awarded the Victoria Cross and survived. Lance Corporal Jackson, not content with his first heroic assault, continued to dominate his part of the battle, to be killed later clearing out an enemy trench. He lies in plot II row D Grave 4. A young officer lies in plot I row A Grave 7, Second Lieutenant Hugh de Barry Cordes MC, aged 19, of the Scots Guards, killed in the same assault. There is another 'old man' in plot II row D Grave 6, Private Albert Davies, aged 40, of the Coldstream. A Grenadier aged 29, Private Thomas Bayliss, killed in the same action, came from the village I have lived in for the past 35 years. His cottage still exists at 5 Victoria Gardens, Hucclecote, now a suburb of Gloucester. Sadly his name is not recorded on the Village War Memorial. I have reported this to all who should be interested and am waiting for his name to be added to the three dozen there now.

**Lance Corporal
Thomas Norman Jackson VC**

This tour has covered the capture of the western end of Flesquières Ridge. The capture of Graincourt by Bradford's 186 Brigade is described in the **Battleground** guide *Bourlon Wood* in this series. On its village green there are some military trophies. Drive through the village towards the main N30 road – it does not matter which of the two roads you take – but when you arrive at it, somewhere near the village of Anneux and the south-west corner of Bourlon Wood, is where the German column was ambushed in the dark on 20 November 1917 by Second Lieutenant Castle's platoon of the Dukes.

Private HH Horsfall.

TOUR TWO

This tour covers the arrival of the tank Battalions H and B from Dessart Wood, 71 Brigade of the 6th Division and the attack on Ribécourt and the eastern end of the Flesquières Ridge. Finally, north-east to Premy Chapel and Noyelles sur Escaut.

Battle Maps: 5, 7, 13, 14, 15.   Tour circuit distance: **25 miles**.

Assuming you have stayed at Cambrai, drive down the N44, the Paris road, it is about eleven miles to the start of the tour at Gouzeaucourt. En route you cross the battlefields of the right flank battles for the bridges over the St Quentin Canal on 20 November 1917, covered in *Cambrai: the Right Hook*. The long straight road we are on is the southern edge of the bowl; in due course a major fork in the road at Bonavis is reached. There is a restaurant on the left and opposite, at the fork, is Bonavis Farm, where Bed and Breakfast accommodation is available in the historic building.

Take the right fork, driving along the bottom edge of the bowl, the Flanders Sanatorium, all part of the Cambrai battlefield. Go over the autoroute (on the right is the tiny hamlet of La Vacquerie, on the top of Welch Ridge, the scene of bitter fighting as the British broke through the Hindenburg Line) and continue on to Gouzeaucourt.

For a small diversion, take the main road, the D917 to Fins, which runs south west from the village to Dessart Wood, three miles away. It is from here that H, B, and A Tank Battalions, laid up after unloading at Ytres, set out for the battle area we are going to see. There is nothing to see except three small woods.

Return to the village and take the D29 towards Trescault and Havrincourt. The tour now follows the path of tanks and the infantry of the 6th Division. Within a mile, over on the left **(1)**, is Dead Man's Corner, a place of some significance in the March and September 1918 battles. At **(2)** there is a track going to the right where 18 Brigade waited to advance at mid morning on the 20th and to **(4)**, where H Battalion was lined up, engines ticking over in the dark, ready for the attack. It was here that Elles, the Tank Corps Commander, came (along with his makeshift flag) and told the tank commander of *Hilda* that he was going into battle with him. Imagine the scene here that morning: rows of tanks, exhaust smoke curling up from the engines; excited crews having their last breath of fresh air before getting into the hulls; and about 3,000 infantry filing past them, heading for the jump off trenches about Beaucamp. The lines of artillery lay further back, ready to fire their stunning unregistered barrage. This now tranquil hill top was alive with thousands of men, many of whom would not see another dawn. Of course, further over to the left, were 10,000 more men – the Highlanders with their tanks and we have seen the ground of the West Yorkshire Division already on the left flank in Havrincourt Wood. Some 60,000 men, 1,000 guns and 400 tanks were crammed into a stretch of land not more than five miles long and two miles deep, all about to pounce on the unsuspecting Germans.

At **(3)**, Charing Cross, turn right for Beaucamp **(5)** and proceed slowly. Trescault is about a mile to the left. The view over the valley, the Bowl, of the battlefield to Flesquières is really lovely now and normally Cambrai is visible in the far distance. Drive slowly into the tiny hamlet, it was really nothing more than a large farm, but new houses have sprung

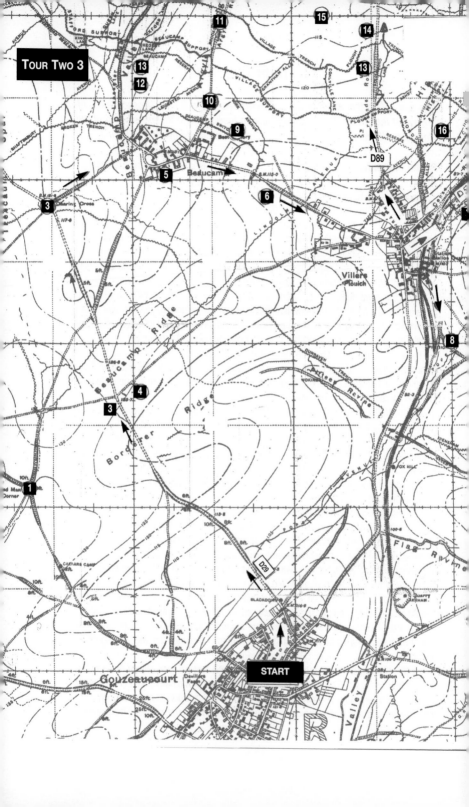

up in the last few years, turn right at the T junction and stop.

It is time to walk and consult the battle maps and re-read the story. There is a small addition to the main narrative. On 27 September 1918 (the Germans had reoccupied this front edge of the Hindenburg Line in March 1918) the Lancashire Fusiliers of 125 Brigade, the right flank of the 42nd (East Lancashire) Division, launched an attack at Trescault in a most audacious advance against the Hindenburg Line without tanks. The brigade passed in front of Beaucamp, taking its front face, whilst elements of the 5th Division attacked it full on. It would not fall to them and in consequence 125 Brigade was hit hard by machine gun fire. With repeated and heroic attacks the village finally fell. You will see the graves of the Fusiliers in the cemeteries in this and the third tour. Here in 1917, November, 71 Brigade waited to advance.

On either side of you were trenches; a short walk to the left brings you to a pumping station, site of the brigade's left flank. The Leicesters and the Norfolks came through here, heading for Ribécourt in the valley bottom. The Battle Map **(13)** gives you the location and names of some of the trenches. On the other side of the hamlet, that is go to the right at the 'T' junction, the main road curves and 100 yards or so will bring you to a bus shelter, a telephone box and a track on the left. Follow the track, which starts off with a hard surface but becomes a rough track. Whilst it can be negotiated by a car it is not recommended. This was Argyll Road **(10)**, the centre line for 71 Brigade's attack. Imagine the tanks coming forward behind the artillery barrage, fighter planes flying low overhead and machine gunning the enemy trenches about 600 yards distant. Walk for that distance down the track to **(11)** on the battlefield, and re-read the story. You can see **(12)** where the Leicesters waited to be first 'over the top' and **(13)**, the British front line running across your front. The tour will approach Argyll Road from the other end later. Turn round, if you are walking, after about 200 yards and go back to your car. However, if your car can take it there is nothing to stop you from driving to the bottom. Very close to the top of this track Argyll Road on the right, east, is where Captain Brown of the Sherwood Foresters was killed as he laid wooden bridges down to facilitate men crossing the trenches **(9)**, the first man of the battalion to be killed that day. Over on the right, in front of Beaucamps, where the gardens of houses now are, was the site of Argyll Road Cemetery, the original burial ground of the casualties.

Drive slowly down the main, sunken, road and stop at **(6)** Sunken Road British Cemetery. It was along this lane that some of the brigade waited to move into the trenches and later more elements of the 6th Division were here, about to go forward. It was a safe place from bombardment. The bank on the left of the road was full of dugouts, now filled in, but one can discern where they were, often a small bush grows out of the infilling, This small cemetery holds only 51 men with three unknown. It is seemingly not often visited, so spare a moment for them. In grave A 1 lies Second Lieutenant HH Hall of the Sherwood Foresters, who died of wounds on 2 December 1917. You will see a number of King's Shropshire Light Infantry men killed in the great German counter-attack of 30 November. Proceed into the village of Villers-Plouich, which features many times in the story of the Hindenburg Line. At the bottom turn left, past the church and over the railway line, onto the D56 to Marcoing. Within a few yards you will see the communal cemetery **(7)** on the right, at the foot of Welch Ridge The visit here is to two casualties of the fighting in the area covered in this book. Private William Harris of 2/York and Lancs was killed in 16 Brigade's attack, part of the 6th Division, heading along this road for Marcoing. He lies in row A Grave 13. Close to him, in Grave 7, is a tank gunner, ST Morgan of B Battalion, also attacking Marcoing.

Before leaving look at the map, noting **(16)**, **(17)** and **(18)**. **(16)** is where the cavalry assembled in the afternoon of the 20th, hoping for the great breakthrough which never came. **(17)** marks the line of 16 Brigade's advance that day when the two young men whose graves we have seen were killed, and **(18)** is where the main Hindenburg Line crossed the British front. Behind the cemetery is a track running parallel to the road. The track, a mile or so long, was Surrey Road, one of the British trenches for the attack up the hill by the 12th Division that same morning. The scene before us is of a major attack against the Hindenburg Line, with dozens of tanks going over the slope. Two Victoria Crosses were won up there that morning.

Turn left out of the cemetery, back into the village and very quickly take the left turn over the railway line on the D89 for Gonnelieu. After some fifty yards you will see a sign pointing to the right down a narrow track to **(8)** 15 Ravine Cemetery, about 200 yards away. Turning around there is no problem but perhaps you would prefer to park in the open space on the left of the road. If you have driven down the track and parked at the junction of a number of 'hollows' near the cemetery gate, the end of Surrey Road and where three communication trenches met are easily seen. The cemetery's name is derived from fifteen trees which once bordered the shallow ravine.

It is an important cemetery for the battles against the Hindenburg Line. It was begun in April 1917, when the Welsh battalions of the 40th Division came here, forcing the enemy back behind their main line. It continued to be used by the British until the Germans recaptured the area in March 1918; the British regained it in the October. It contains 1,139 men (740 unknown), but in March 1918 there were only 107 graves here.

Captain Ernest Brown (see **(9)** above) of the 2nd Sherwood Forester's lies in plot IV row H Grave 11. That plot is on the left of the War Stone, to the left of the gate. There are two Army Chaplains in row C, three from the front, both killed with the men they were sure to be comforting on 1 December 1917. Reverend Holden lies in grave **15** and next to him is Reverend Howell. Many of 71 Brigade lie here in plot IV. In row H Grave 20, close to Captain Brown, is a young captain, the holder of the MC and Bar, fighting with the 11/Essex. Sydney Edwin Silver was married to Jose and lived in Forest Gate, London. Next to him is Second Lieutenant AK Purdy, aged 23, serving with the 1/Leicester's, no doubt killed in the same attack on Ribécourt. Just six graves away is Private Fred Ingate of the 11/Essex. If you move to plot II, directly in front of the War Stone, there are many more from 71 Brigade, presumably concentrated here after the war.

There are Lancashire casualties here also from the 42nd (East Lancs) Division's capture of Flesquières Ridge in the last battle of September 1918. For example, Sergeant Harry Pulford of the Manchesters killed on the 29th (plot VII row C Grave 2), who is three rows away from the interesting Argyll Special Memorial against the left hand wall.

Return to the village and just behind the colourful Mairie note the plaque 'twinning' the village with Wandsworth.

Turn sharp left in front of the church, the road to Ribécourt and climb the hill to Highland Ridge. Stop at the peak of the road, where it is high banked on the right **(13)**, and get out. The view of the battlefields on both sides of the road is good, the road being about the centre line of the whole 6th Division, 16 Brigade on the right and the 71st (the interest on this tour) on the left. Coming from left to right out of the Trescault Ridge on 27

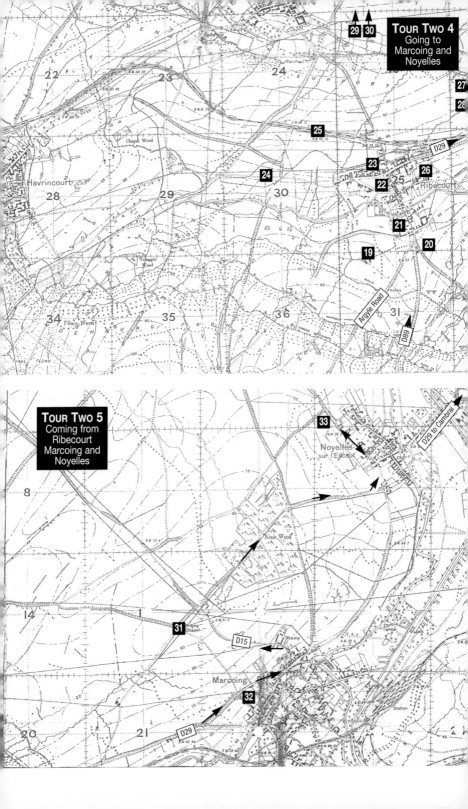

TOUR TWO 4
Going to Marcoing and Noyelles

TOUR TWO 5
Coming from Ribecourt Marcoing and Noyelles

Captain Blackwell DSO
20 November 1917.

6th Division's battlefield 20 November 1917.

September 1918 was the 42nd (East Lancs) Division. One can see once more where the Lancashire Fusiliers were cut up in front of Beaucamp **(5)**. **(14)** indicates the area of the advance of the Robin Hoods; further, on the left **(15)** is where Elles was ditched in *Hilda*. Leaving it, he walked back through the shell and bullet swept battleground and up the hill to where he had started out that morning.

Proceed slowly now and Ribécourt comes into view. At the bottom of the hill **(20)** stop at Ribécourt British Cemetery. It was started by the 6th Division after its battle in November 1917 but it was used again at intervals until March 1918 and again in September and October 1918. It is long and narrow – almost arrow head shaped – with the rows of graves quite difficult to locate without the cemetery map. There are 290 graves (18 unknown); but against the wall are the headstones of 81 men whose graves were destroyed by subsequent shellfire and who are now remembered by Special Memorials. You will find men from 1917, particularly the 6th Division, more than eighty of them, and at least 21 from the two Tank Corps Battalions, B and E. Also there are many gunners and Royal Engineers and the 42nd Division's action here in September/October 1918 is also indicated. Walk along the wall to see the Special Memorials. I always think how very sad it is that these men, buried once by their comrades, are now lost forever. No.42 is that to Second Lieutenant T.R. Wilson, aged 22, killed whilst commanding Exquisite, a wire crusher of E Battalion; near him in Memorial No.36 is Second Lieutenant G. Testi who commanded *Egypt*, No. E17. He was killed in the same encounter. At the top, in the centre, is the long row D in plot I; there you will find in Grave 11 Reverend RJ Monteith, aged 40, and at the start of the same row in grave 1 is the oldest man here, aged 42, Gunner J.H. Cole killed in a tank from E Battalion at the north east of the village when the tanks were cruelly dealt with by a battery of 77mm Field Guns waiting for the long line of tanks approaching up the hill. There are many young men, nineteen and twenty years old, but the youngest is Private GL Sumsion, aged eighteen, of the Norfolks, remembered on Special Memorial No.8 to the left of the gate. In row B, to the left of D, closer to the left wall, in grave 12 is Captain RS Whitmore MC, aged 23, of the KSLI. There is a 20 year old Naval Officer in plot I row F grave 8, Lieutenant DE Maloney from Tipperary was killed in the Naval Division's defence of the

Serjeant J Whelan
20 November 1917.

Gunner J H Cole
20 November 1917

Flesquières salient in March 1918. In row B on the left side of plot I, lying in Grave 5, is a remarkable young man, aged 27, Second Lieutenant HF Amesbury. He was born into an Army family in India, served with the 1st Canadian Division at Ypres and on the Somme, was wounded at Thiepval and killed here leading his company of Bedfords on 27 November 1917.

Take the track opposite the cemetery, heading towards Beaucamp and drive for a few hundred yards up the hill. You are at the bottom of Argyll Road. Stop when you are opposite **(19)**. There was a double machine gun bunker in the last row of defences of the Hindenburg Line which was quickly eliminated. Turn around now and look at Battle Map 14 and with Ribécourt before you, read the story of its capture.

Drive back, down to the village. On the left is **(21)** where the Norfolks attacked and secured the two bridges; **(22)** is the rebuilt, fortified church. You might care to park here and walk in order to see better features of the battle. Going north, just beyond the cross roads, was the site of the railway station and 71 Brigade's boundary. If you turn left at a crossroads you are in the Grand Ravine valley. Above is **(25)**, the railway embankment which featured in 71 Brigade's and the 51st Highland Division's attacks (see Tour 3). Once more in your car, turn right to **(26)**, Railway Cemetery. The Blue line was also here.

Re-read the battle account. Before you go in to the cemetery look towards **(27)**; the 11th Essex fought their way to here.

The cemetery is very small and frequently overlooked, holding only 53 graves, one of them unknown. It was made by the 3rd Division in September/October 1918. There are only four rows, A, B, C, and D, A being on the left of the gate. There are a number of very young men here – conscripts or perhaps over eager volunteers. In row A Grave 5 is the youngest, aged 18, Private William Livesey of the King's Liverpools, leaving parents at 78 Prospect Street, Lancaster. Pioneer CT Fletcher, originally a sapper but transferred to the 70th Labour Company, was killed on 8 October 1918. Obviously an older man, he came from Gosport, leaving his widow, Ethel Florence, there at 126 Priory Road. There are two sergeants of 1/HLI, Peter Dolman MM and Bar and Thomas Johnston MM. Sergeant Dolman was killed on 1 October 1918 and Sergeant Johnston died of wounds two days later, no doubt both casualties from the same attack. There is also a sergeant a long way from home. Lying in row B Grave 9 is Joseph Leonard Benton, aged 24, from New Zealand who died of wounds on 1 October. His New Zealand Division leap frogged the 42nd Division in September 1918. As you leave pause at the first grave on the left of the gate, Private Saville Walker MM, aged 21, one of the unsung heroes of the RAMC, serving

Private J W Trundle
Gloucestershire Regt.

159

with the 8th Field Ambulance when he was killed on 7 October 1918.

Turn right at the gate to **(28)**. Crossing the road here was Kaiser Trench, part of the Hindenburg Support Line. The track on the left is all that remains here. **(29)** and **(30)** respectively indicate Flesquières Hill Cemetery and the Sugar Beet Factory at Flesquières. They will be visited in Tour 3.

Drive into the north-western end of Marcoing on the D29. Just on the edge of the village **(32)** is the Communal Cemetery where there is another group of British graves often overlooked. It was first used by the Germans in 1917 but their 129 men were removed in 1919 to Cambrai (Tour 5). There were eight British PoWs, but they have been reinterred at St Souplet, near Le Cateau. This small group here includes thirteen unknown and eleven Special Memorials to men whose graves were subsequently lost during the Cambrai battle; four men are known, the youngest of whom is 19 years old Second Lieutenant Yates of the Hampshires.

Turn right, further along the edge of the village and then turn left on the D15, heading for Premy Chapel **(31)**, the extreme end of Flesquières Ridge and where 18 Brigade of the 6th Division followed through after 71 Brigade had taken the ridge. Turn right through Nine Wood and drive on to Noyelles-sur-Escaut. The account of the fighting in this village is told in *Cambrai the Right Hook*, however we have come here to see some massive German bunkers and another small cemetery **(33)**. The bunkers were used as ammunition stores and barracks and in 1918 a large number of the enemy here were caught asleep by the British. Opposite the bunkers is another communal cemetery extension which is rarely visited. There is only one Briton in the Communal section, in the bottom left hand corner. Lieutenant WB Cramb of the RFC was buried here by the Germans on 14 April 1917. There are 115 graves (only 4 unknown) in the British Extension. For the most part they are from the 2nd, 62nd and the 63rd Divisions, who fell in the advance to victory in September and October 1918. Private M Tester was one of the thirty-six men of the 17th Royal Fusiliers killed in crossing the St Quentin Canal here on 28/29 September 1918. He was from East Grinstead and must have been very underage when he enlisted; as he was only seventeen when he was killed (row A Grave 9. Nearby is Private ME Tickner, aged thirty-six, of 24/Royal Fusiliers, whose wife lived in Paddock Wood but whose parents were in Carlisle, Concord Lowell, USA. There must be an interesting personal story here.

You can return to Cambrai either by the shortest and most direct route, the D29, back into the village and turn left for the church and then the bridge over the canal or take the road past the cemetery, the D142, towards Cantaing-sur-Escaut then to Fontaine-Notre-Dame and the N30.

Noyelles German artillery bunkers.

TOUR THREE

This tour covers the arrival of the tank Battalions E and D from the south-east corner of Havrincourt Wood and the 51st Highland Division's attack on the centre of the Flesquières Ridge.

Battle Maps: 4, 5, 7, 11, 16, 17, 18.   Tour circuit distance: **18 miles**.

Assuming you have stayed in Cambrai, then drive down the N30 for about 11 miles until you see the road on the left to Beaumetz-les-Cambrai, the D18E, the same route as Tour 1. Go through the village and follow the road to Vélu Wood and take the road round it to the right. My father told me that whilst serving here in the 42nd (East Lancs) Division in the spring of 1917 and the autumn of 1918, that he actually tied his two horses, Ellerby and Lily, to the same tree. In 1917 the wood was a terrible place, still filled with dead horses and Germans from their withdrawal to the Hindenburg Line just a few miles further east. However in 1918 it had been cleaned up and the chateau, very much repaired, was used by 42nd Division as its Headquarters. Continue to Bertincourt, but keep to this road, going through the western edge of the village and following the signs for Ytres. The road will cross the old railway junction where the tanks of G Battalion and, on the right, a few hundred yards away E and D Battalions unloaded. Of course the railway lines have gone but if you were walking the old line can easily be recognised. Enter Ytres; at its north-east corner; **(7)** is where Major General Harper had his Highland Division's HQ, perhaps too far from his battle. Following the road, with the church on your right, until at the southern end of the village continue towards Péronne (the D43), a large town fifteen miles away. Go slowly; by coming this way round to the battle you get an appreciation of the distances involved for the tanks and marching infantry.

On the left **(2)** you will see the railway station buildings where H and B Tank Battalions were unloaded and **(6)** is the start of the two mile tunnel for the Canal du Nord, which will be seen later. At a minor road on the right, the D19E, you will see about 500

The ruined railway station at Ytres today. The entrance to the Canal du Nord tunnel is a few yards behind this building.

yards away, in the middle of the field, the Cross of Sacrifice of Five Points Cemetery **(3)**, turn up the road and visit it. I doubt if many visitors come here. It contains only 100 graves and only three are unknown. This is because it was made by the 53rd Field Ambulance and the 18th Casualty Clearing Station sited nearby. Imagine the people, the nurses, ambulance drivers, horses, vehicles, tents and huts filling this field. To the south, on the main road, one can see another cemetery.

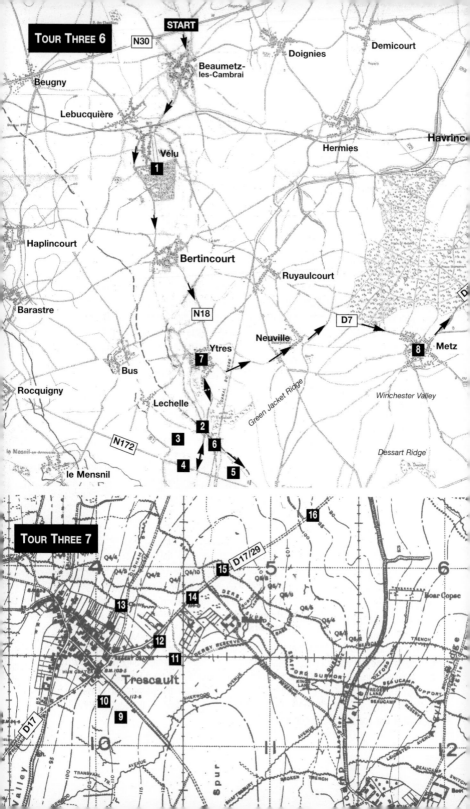

Brigadier General ARC Sanders CMG, DSO.

Driver Dina.

There are two graves of particular note. In row D Grave 6 is Brigadier General A.R.C. Sanders CMG, DSO and Bar, Legion of Honour, a Royal Engineer officer aged 41 who was commanding 50 Brigade of the 17th Division when he was mortally wounded on 20 September 1918. Near him, at the opposite end of the social scale, is the only Indian soldier buried here, Driver Dina, serving with the 38th Division Artillery Column. He died of wounds on 16 September 1918. I wonder if his wife, Pullam, at Rohat Sonipat Rohtak in the Punjab, ever knew how he died or where he was buried. Another man from my father's Battery (but a Londoner) lies in row A Grave 20. Gunner CH Thwaites was twenty-three when he was killed 8 October 1918.

Return to your car and drive back and then turn right at the junction, up the hill on the road from Ytres railway station to the crossroads at the D112; as you climb the hill you can see **(4)** the large cemetery on the right, near the corner. It is Rocquigny-Equancourt British Cemetery. You can park alongside the wall in the recess there. It was made by the 21st and 48th Casualty Clearing Stations and men were brought here from many parts of the Hindenburg Line battlefield. It was started in 1917 and used until March 1918, but burials were resumed here in the autumn of 1918. The register records 1,838 graves – only 22 are unknown. It is very large and you will need the register in the safe at the gate. I usually sit on the stone seat for a while and just look at this scene of human tragedy hidden by the beauty of the cemetery itself. Perhaps a cup of coffee is a good idea whilst you look through the register for men you wish to visit. Under a tree, only a few yards from the gate against the wall alongside the road lining the cemetery, in plot III row E grave 1, lies Sergeant Rhodes VC, DCM and Bar, aged 26, of the 3/Grenadier Guards, who was mortally wounded in front of Fontaine-Notre-Dame on 27 November 1917. He had been awarded the Victoria Cross for bravery at Ypres only some weeks earlier. Over the many years that I have visited I have seen the small tree, which now shades his grave, grow from a tiny sapling.

There are many men here from the Cambrai battle of November 1917. In plot II row C Grave 4 is Second Lieutenant William Muir Clark, aged 19, of the 1/7th Black Watch, killed in the attack on Flesquières Ridge on 20 November. He came from Hawthorne, California. There is a pilot not far from him in row B grave 16, Lieutenant WC Davy of the 15th Squadron RFC, killed on 21 November. There is a notable gentleman in plot VI row B Grave 11, Private The Lord Edward Beauchamp Seymour, aged thirty-eight, of

Serjeant Rhodes VC, DCM and Bar.

163

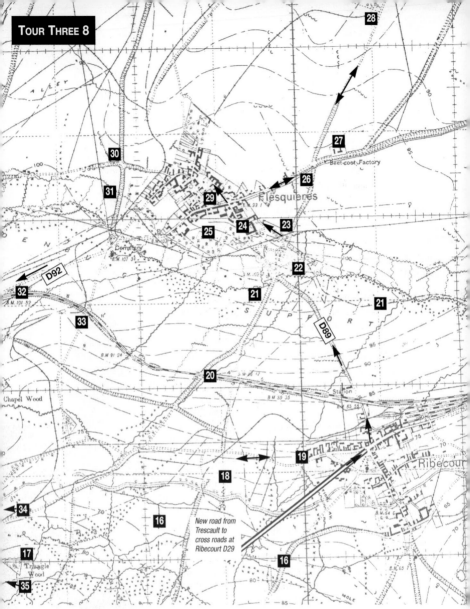

Lord Strathcona's Horse, dying of wounds here 5 December 1917. He was the son of the 6th Marquis of Hertford and husband of Lady Seymour of Worcester. I wonder why he chose to serve in the ranks in a Canadian cavalry regiment. There is another highly decorated young man in plot IV row D Grave 9, Second Lieutenant JW Worth MC, DCM, commissioned from the ranks into the West Yorks. At the age of twenty-six he died of wounds received at Havrincourt with the 62nd Division. Drive down the main road to **(5)** the bridge you can see, half a mile away. There you have a good view of the Canal du Nord and the entrance to the tunnel. Just beyond the bridge, now a site of a stone quarry, was

164

where fuel for the rockets and flying bombs which bombarded London during the Second World War was made.

Return to Ytres and take the minor road to Neuville-Bourjonval then turn right at the cross roads on the corner of Havrincourt Wood and go to Metz. At **(8)** the ruined village of Metz sheltered the 51st Highland Division before going into the assault on Flesquières. Turn left at a crossroads, once a large mine crater and proceed on the D17 towards Trescault. Along here came not only tanks – which would lead them – but infantrymen of the 51st (Highland) Division from their billets in the ruined village. The tour passes where 154 brigade waited to go into action in the early hours of the 21st. Perhaps it is time to stop and re-read the account of 152 and 153 Brigades' attack and look at the battle maps 17 and 18.

As you near Trescault, stop at the crossroads. To the right you will see **(9)** and **(10)**, where D and E Tank Battalions waited, with engines running, in the dark before leading the advance down the valley side, through the massive barbed wire fences of the Hindenburg Line and into the Grand Ravine. Drive in the village along the road to Ribécourt and park at the battle scarred memorial **(12)** to the 42nd (East Lancashire) Division, put here in recognition of their magnificent assault and capture of the Hindenburg Line on 27 September 1918. 'Their' cemetery **(14)** is a few yards down the road and here is **(12)** Bilhem Farm. Stand here and view the battlefield with the help of the maps. You can see Flesquières high on the ridge, the Grand Ravine down below and on the far horizon the spires of Cambrai. <u>The view from here, between the memorial and Ribecourt Road Cemetery, is the most comprehensive of any when seeing the Battle of Cambrai</u>. To your

right, high on the ridge, is Beaucamps, first taken by the 40th Division's Welsh battalions in the spring of 1917. In front of it you can see the battlefield of the Lancashire Fusiliers in September 1918, cut up by the German machine guns in the village, which should have been taken by the 5th Division. 450 Lancashire Fusiliers had started out from the line of the modern D15 road which you crossed to get here and only 150 were left fighting at the end of the day. Bilhem Farm, now behind the Memorial, is where the cavalry had its HQ on the morning of the 20th. At **(11)** were the 2,000 men of 152 Brigade, Seaforths, Gordons and Argylls, in the trenches across the sloping land to your right; the track in front of the copse on the right was one of them. At **(13)** was 153 Brigade (Gordons and Black Watch), their trenches to the left of this, the Ribécourt road. Running across the road at about the position of the cemetery was the British

The author and the 42nd East Lancs Division memorial at Trescault. Behind is Bilhem Farm where the cavalry had its HQ on the morning of 20 November 1917.

front line **(15)** and beyond it the start of the Hindenburg Line's almost 800 yards depth of barbed wire and trenches, going down to the bottom of the valley. There are two cemeteries to visit here, the large one ahead on the right and the village cemetery. Walk back towards the village and take the first sharp right turn down to the cemetery. There are only seven men here. All except one was killed when the British were first here in the spring of 1917, following the enemy back to his line. The 'odd man out' is Lieutenant Nathaniel Arthur Pierce of 4/Grenadier Guards, aged 21, from Wellington, New Zealand. He was killed on 25 November 1917 as the Guards went forward to their attack on Fontaine-Notre-Dame.

Standing here you are on the extreme left flank of 153 Brigade's attack towards Flesquières Ridge and where Trescault Support Trench was. You have a splendid view of the brigade's attack. Go back now and drive to the large cemetery, **(14)** Ribécourt Road Cemetery, where there are 261 graves (nine unknown). This is because more than half of the men here are from the 42nd (East Lancs) Division's battle here on 27 September 1918, the other 117 men were part of the occupation of the Flesquières salient prior to 21 March 1918. In plot II row B Grave 1, in front of the Great Cross, is the commander of *Ella* No.27, Second Lieutenant WS Haining, aged 23. The most decorated man, who from his long service with the Territorial Division in Egypt, Gallipoli, Sinai, Ypres, and all points on the Western Front must surely have thought he would get home safely, is Private George Heard DCM, MM, of the Lancashire Fusiliers, aged 33, from Manchester, killed on 27 September 1918: he lies in plot IV row B Grave 1. In plot **(1)** row A Grave 2 is a gunner who joined up fifty numbers senior to my father in the Burnley Battery. Joseph Lee came from Hardy Street, he and my dad probably walked home from the barracks together many times before they left for Egypt in September 1914.

Drive down as far as the pumping station, you are near to **(16)**, the German Main Line. Somewhere close to your right was where *Ella*, Tank 27, was knocked out. In the land to your left and deep into the Hindenburg Line were seven tanks that became stuck in the deep trenches and wire and were then abandoned. Of course the whole landscape was filled with advancing men, incoming machine gun fire and shell bursts, whilst Flesquières Ridge in front of you would have been obscured by the British smoke bombardment. On the right was 152 Brigade battling through the wire and further over was 71 Brigade. Thousands of men going forward with the single aim of 'Flesquières Ridge that morning' (apart from the need to survive, of course!). To the left, about a mile away, is Triangle Wood **(17)** and at **(35)** Grand Ravine Cemetery. A few more yards further across the valley and the tour moves out of the 51st (Highland) Division's sector, 71 Brigade here going for Ribécourt. 152 Brigade was advancing, virtually along the track running down from the pumping station, into the Grand Ravine **(18)**.

Continue; turn left at the crossroads in Ribécourt. Drive as far as you can, then walk (Please do not feel venturous; I have managed this track all the way in a car, but frequently wished that I had not started and there are no good turning points!). Certainly with the Battle Map 18 you will get a better feel. Stop at **(19)**. About here Lance Corporal McBeath charged towards Ribécourt to eliminate a machine gun post, thereby winning the VC. At **(20)** was a communication trench, Ravine Alley.

Imagine the thousands of men and dozens of tanks filling this narrow defile after their triumphant attack down into the valley, refuelling and resting exploring the many splendid German dugouts with their booty of wine and cigars the very many enemy dead along the ravine and slopes with parties of prisoners being marched away. Re-read here the story of the next phase of the attack, which was most costly in men and tanks. The travelling

German bunker on the western edge of Ribécourt which McBeath charged towards the camera from beyond the farm and wiped out the Germans manning it. He was awarded the VC. The farm was not built then.

distance to Flesquières is short but there is much to read and see. Before turning round look at **(33)**, it was Cemetery Alley and is not far away. The trench system which you can see was dug for the BBC programmes, *The Trench* and cuts across it; the railway embankment **(32)** goes across the valley slope in front of you. Look up the track to **(21)**, it is not far to walk. The Hindenburg Support Line ran across here in front of the ridge top.

Turn around, go back and rejoin your car, go into Ribécourt (Tour 2) and drive up the hill, the D89. Go slowly, for here at the top of the road, roughly where a track runs off to the left **(22)** was the scene of E Battalion's disaster at the hands of a battery of German 77mm field guns firing in an anti-tank role. The whole area here and to the right of this road was littered with more than a dozen tanks, most suffering from direct hits, their crews burnt to death. Stop and walk to the right where the road is sunken and just beyond is a narrow strip of wood jutting out of the main wood of the chateau into the open fields. Here are demolished German bunkers. In 1917 it was only a very thin stand of blasted and ruined trees but just behind, in the middle of the field, was the German gun battery **(23)**, waiting for the tanks to appear out of the sunken road and to destroy each one as it came into view. There are two concrete, complete, German bunkers just behind the trees. Stop at the cross roads with the imposing gates of Chateau Farm on the corner. There will be an imposing monument here to the Tank Corps. The tank that Philippe Gorczynski and his team of enthusiasts excavated (*Deborah* No. D51) is securely housed in a barn a few yards away. Behind the long brick wall of Chateau Farm (in private property!), twenty five yards through the gate, on the left, there are still purpose built concrete and cylindrical metal machine gun posts from the battle and the entrance to a tunnel leading to the machine gun bunker 200 yards in front of the wall on the crest of the ridge which one can see it amongst the crop. It is easy to see why they caused carnage to the attacking Highlanders held up by the uncut barbed wire crossing the fields in front of you. The Hindenburg

167

Direction of attacking Highlanders

Flesquières Chateau wall – original as in 1917. German machine gun posts looking towards attacking highlanders.

Support Line is all about you here. Leaving Chateau Farm **(24)** continue into the village and stop at the village green on the left **(29)**, where there are two memorials, one to nineteen French soldiers burnt to death in 1940, the other to an American soldier. Corporal Johannes Borgman was commanding a patrol of the US 113 Reconnaissance Squadron and was the first Allied soldier to enter the village on 2 September 1944. Many photographs were taken of the few American liberators, the delighted villagers surrounding his jeep and an armoured car. Later that day his small column left and on the road to Cantaing, close to the Sugar Beet Factory, he was shot by a sniper and killed. He was brought back into the village and taken to the church and buried in the cemetery, the whole village following his coffin. In 1948 his family came to take him home and he was reinterred at Oak Hill, Parkers Burg, Iowa. He is remembered here every September.

1/6th Seaforths got into these streets in the dusk of the 20th but had to withdraw, the tanks unable to help them. Quite close to here at the crossroads was where the recently recovered *Deborah*, Second Lieutenant FG Heap's tank, was knocked out and abandoned. The Germans subsequently removed it for possible future use an underground shelter on the outskirts of the village.

Go now to Flesquières Hill Cemetery **(26)**, a few hundred yards east of the green. It holds 914 men (352 unknown). Incidentally if you did not see the site of the German anti-tank Battery it is about 300 yards south-east of the cemetery in the middle of a field. The cemetery was made from six other battlefield burial grounds: Flesquières, Marcoing, Masnières and other places; 668 men came from these and they were originally buried

Looking down Flesquières ridge towards the attacking Highlanders. An undergroung passage leads from the German bunker to a point behind the wall.

Beaucamp Ridge

German bunker

German machine guns firing from behind wall

on the site of the old German cemetery, where plots III and VIII now are. This concentration of graves accounts for the great variety of regiments and nations found here, including men from New Zealand, Newfoundland, Canada, Guernsey, Australia and Great Britain. As you would expect there are a number of Tank Corps men here in known graves (16 of them), but there must be many more in the unknown graves, burnt beyond recognition. The Corps' losses in the Cambrai battle were about 240 and the Ridge accounted for a great many of them. The Memorial at Louverval (Tour 4) to the 7,000 missing of the battle remembers about 160 of them. Lance Corporal GC Foot DCM, only twenty years old, of D Battalion, was killed 20 of November and now lies in plot III row B Grave 6. More of his comrades lie in the same plot. In plot IV row C Grave 15 is a 28 year old New Zealander, Private LC King from Ohaeawai, captured whilst serving with the 15th Battalion Australian Infantry and dying as a prisoner of war on 4 February 1917. He must first have been buried elsewhere by the Germans and reinterred after the war. Perhaps the longest serving other ranker here is Farrier Sergeant Thomas Wiseman, aged 33, of the 18th Hussars, lying in plot VIII row I Grave 2. He held the Long Service and Good Conduct Medal for 18 years unblemished service. He was killed on 21 November 1917 and must have enlisted as a boy. There are so many men who were decorated, the Distinguished Conduct Medal and the Military Medal are shown on many graves. There is one in plot VIII row G Grave 1, Lance Bombardier Harold Gilbert DCM, aged 28, of the RFA killed on 29 September 1918, only six weeks away from the Armistice. There is an 'old sailor' in plot V row C Grave 13, aged 42, from the Isle of Wight, killed fighting as an infantryman on 30 December 1917, A B IEO Johnson, a RNVR man serving with Drake Battalion RND. There are many of his shipmates here. In plot I row D Grave 1 is Lieutenant Colonel RS Walker DSO, aged 46, of the Royal Engineers, who had served on the Western Front since 1914. In plot VIII row E Grave 10 lies Second Lieutenant RA Jones, killed when commanding

German Hindenburg Line bunker

Trescault Ridge

Behind the Chateau wall is the entrance to tunnels which lead to German bunkers.

Devil II, Tank No.D41, on 20 November 1917, almost certainly in his battalion's attack on the western end of Flesquières, we will see the spot later in the tour.

Go to the mid point at the back of the cemetery and peer across the field to the walls of Chateau Farm beyond the field. You should be able to make out a German signalling bunker built into the wall. Then go to a position in the cemetery where you have a good view of the northern Cambrai battlefield and in particular the massive German counter-attack against Flesquières on 30 November 1917 and their great offensive of March 1918 as they strove to eliminate the salient. However, also 'see' the Guard Division sweeping towards you, from the left, after crossing the Canal du Nord on 26 September 1918. Notice the dominating position of the Sugar Beet Factory, its machine guns mauling the attackers on that day.

Head towards Orival Wood Cemetery **(28)** about a mile away on the D89 to Anneux, but as you drive past the corner on the sunken section of

German signalling post against Chateau Farm wall.

Guards attack towards Containg

the road stop and read the next few sentences, looking back at the site of the large Sugar Factory where on 6 December 1917 a fierce battle took place in which 2/4th Lincolns and 2/5th Leicesters, with the bayonet, threw the enemy out of the large buildings as they tried to overwhelm the British defences of Flesquières.

On 21 November 1917, 154 Brigade (of Argylls, Seaforths, Gordons and Royal Scots) came forward to seize the abandoned Flesquières and advanced at high cost to the right against Cantaing and Fontaine. On September 27 1918 2/Grenadier Guards finally captured the wood ahead. Drive on now to it.

In 1930 Orival Wood Cemetery was enlarged from its battlefield graves by the concentration of 211 men from Flesquières Chateau Cemetery and the 51st Highland Division's, which was 1,000 yards south of the village near the old railway line. Chateau Cemetery was on the west side of the village. The removal of these cemeteries was highly unusual as one of them was actually fully established with headstones and plantings. The decision to move them was probably made because the land ownership question had not been resolved. On the old site of the 51st Highland Cemetery some of the flowers that were planted in it still flourish. The register here records 284 graves (ten unknown). There are 35 Seaforths, most of whom were killed in the battle for Fontaine. Amongst them is Captain 'Ray' MacDonald DSO, aged 24 (plot I row A Grave 7), killed on the 21st and near him in plot II row B Grave 8 is another Seaforth, Captain GE Edwards DSO, killed attacking up Bourlon Hill. There are 37 Gordons here, nearly all in plot I. The most senior is Captain George Minty, aged 37, from Aberdeen, lying in row A Grave 4. The most senior soldier of the Guards Division lies in plot II row A Grave 13, Major GJM Bagot-Chester of the 2nd Scots Guards, aged 52, would not be left behind at a base job and was killed on 28 November 1917 at Fontaine. There is an enigma in plot II row B Grave 31, Corporal A Bielby, aged twenty, who was killed on 26 December 1917, serving with 10/Lancashire Fusiliers who were not here then; they were with the 17th Division (52nd Brigade) at the German attack in March. There are three Tank Corps men buried in this cemetery.

Return to Flesquières, go round the green, passing between the large church (a very notable piece of post war architecture, which also contains very important stained glass) and the Mairie on the right, and then, following the road round to the left, you are in the area **(31)** of the other major tank disaster, to D Battalion. If you look right toward **(30)**, this was the position of the other German 77mm Field battery that did so much damage. There were at least seven tanks destroyed here; **(21)** shows the line of the Hindenburg Support Line passing in front of the village, see Battle Map 18.

Drive slowly down the D92 towards Havrincourt but stop at the still obvious railway embankment **(32)**. There was much fighting here and there is a magnificent view of the

Flesquières Sugar Factory – a German strong point

Guards attack

Flesquières
Chateau Wood

German anti tank guns

British tanks
advance to
destruction

Direction of
Division's
attack

Sunken
Road

Site of 51st Highland Division's burial ground in 1917.

battlefield of the bowl, the Flanders Sanatorium. If you walk to the railway embankment consider the Highlanders and the tanks fighting their way up the hill, dramatically held up by the impenetrable barbed wire. All round were tanks in trouble. Continue down to Havrincourt and follow the directions to the Grand Ravine cemetery but at the 62nd Division's Memorial park and follow the track to the east. This goes towards Ribécourt along the bottom edge of the Grand Ravine. The track is not good enough for the average car but a walk for 500 to 600 yards takes you along the battlefield of the Highlanders, on both sides of you.

Great rows of barbed wire ran across the valley side to your right with more of the Support line on the left. What a scene it must have been on 20 November, thousands of men on the move, being shelled and shot at, waiting to push on up the hill. You can see Ribécourt in the near distance.

After several hundred yards, up on the left slope you may see the trench system built for the television programme *The Trench*, telling of the deeds of the Hull 'Pals' in 1916; though their battle took place forty miles to the west at Serre. The trench system can be visited by permission of and arrangement with Philippe Gorczynski, the owner of the Hotel Beatus in Cambrai. The system is a good copy of one in the First World War.

Return to Havrincourt, turn left through the village, the D15, go slowly and see the large German Bunker in the bracken at the left hand side of the roads, opposite a red bricked house. Turn left at Trescault, to the left of the church, and return to Ribécourt. To get back to Cambrai, take the D29 to Marcoing and from there to Cambrai.

Deborah **at a barn in Flesquières.**

TOUR FOUR

This tour covers the formation and the defence of the Flesquières salient, 21 March, 1918.

Battle Maps: 19, 24, 25, 26, 27, 28, 29, 30, 31, 32. 33. Tour circuit distance: **23 miles.**

Assuming you have stayed in Cambrai then drive down the N30 for about six miles, going through Fontaine-Notre-Dame, and then the bulk of Bourlon Wood on the right; towards the south-west end of the wood you will see the Cross of Sacrifice at Anneux Cemetery on the left **(1)**. The battle here is covered in the *Battleground* book ***Bourlon Wood***, by the same authors.

Stop for a few minutes and visit this large cemetery, which was not started until October 1918. Remember that the battles here in November and December 1917 left hundreds of dead lying where they fell due to the German advance in December's first week, so many of them in the awful gas sodden wood. The simple, ghastly figures of the cemetery illustrate the situation so clearly: a thousand or so burials (459 unknown); only 131 graves when the cemetery was established and 875 men brought in after the Armistice and only seventy-two named men from the battles here in November and December 1917. It is a most poignant place, not least because so many of the men going into the wood during the fearsome fighting would have passed through, or close to, this piece of land.

Turn left to Anneux and then to Graincourt, where you should park at the village green **(2)**. It is worth re-reading the battle narrative for the 21st November at this point. Walk back to the rebuilt church; there is a small door on the left side, the access to the catacombs which Bradford used as his Brigade's HQ. However it is not possible to see them.

In the approach to the village the battle ground of the 47th (2nd London) Division was crossed as it withdrew from Bourlon Wood in the first week of December 1917. It was around this village that it held the front, the left flank of the Outpost Line, for two days until ordered to withdraw to the main line of defence for the Flesquières salient. The division had suffered terribly during its time on Bourlon Hill; casualties were 3,400 with at least 600 of them 'missing'. A fair number of those men of the London Battalions must lie in Anneux Cemetery.

Take the D15E going south east out of the village. This road was then known as the Yellow Line, to be held until the main line of defences, 2,000 yards behind, was ready. Defending the road were the Londoners. There was minimal cover and they did what they could to scrape hollows in the sunken road. One can see that their field of fire was poor due to the convex shape of the land looking eastwards. Ahead is the complex of the autoroute which covers part of the field of battle of the British withdrawal into the Flesquières salient on 4 – 6 December 1917.

A significant point was at La Justice **(3)**, reached by going underneath the autoroute and, at the 'T' Junction with the D89, turn left, crossing the autoroute this time and stop (safely) at the next road junction, some hundreds of yards further on. Time has altered the road somewhat but here was more of the Outpost Line, held to allow the main resistance to take place to the south-west, on the north east face of Flesquières. La Justice was a

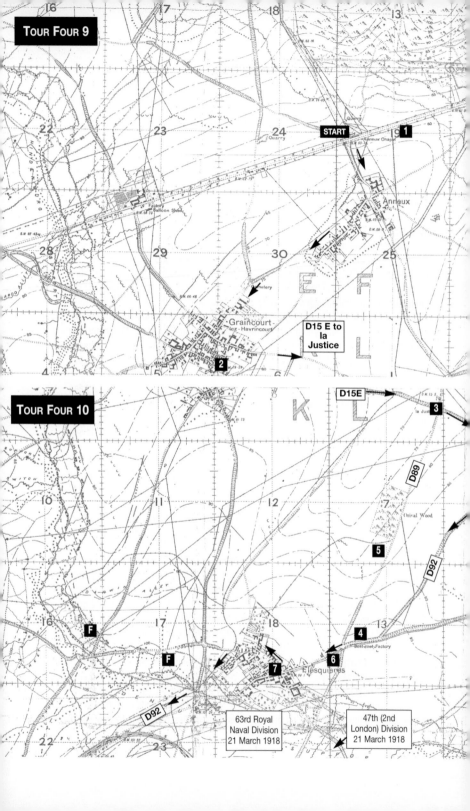

large, battered farm building on the right of the road between the two tracks going right. Both the Germans, who had reinforced it with concrete, and the British used the badly damaged farm as a Dressing Station. The Highlanders, on 21 November 1917, after occupying Flesquières, had used it as a Brigade HQ for the attack on Cantaing and Fontaine. Somewhere along here there was a steep bank and a very big German dugout holding a battalion HQ, whilst others were full of German shells. As the British struggled to dig holes in the ground, frozen to a depth of two feet, wounded stragglers continued to come in. There were hundreds of them, many badly gassed and blinded men, reeling along the track, the medical staff doing their best to treat them at the farm under the persistent shell and machine gun fire.

The autoroute has altered the ground of the Yellow Line but it went to the right at the first T junction **(3)**, then at the next crossroads turned right (D92), running south-westerly to Flesquières. Here were the Sherwood Foresters and the Lincolns doing their utmost to make a defence line. Eventually on 6 December the Germans arrived in force and somewhere on the extreme right, perhaps at the junction with the D92, Lieutenant Hall of 2/7th Sherwoods went forward to see what was going on and was killed. His body was recovered and he now lies in plot II row B Grave 46 in the nearby Orival Wood Cemetery **(5)**. Eventually the Outpost Line had to be given up and the 59th Division withdrew down the tracks, now the D92 and D89, into the Flesquières main line of defence.

At **(4)** is the site of the Sugar Beet Factory, where 2/4th Lincolns and 2/5th Leicesters cleared out the Germans who had occupied it. However the Germans returned and you can get some appreciation just how close the eventual German line to Flesquières was.

Drive close to the village green **(7)** and halt before a turning to the left; there is plenty of space near a bus stop. The ground over which the British withdrew in December 1917 in this area has been seen; now the intention is to look at the left flank of the salient. It is worth looking at the chapter on the defence of the salient in March 1918 and the relevant maps. The Fifth Army was considerably outnumbered, and disorganised by the reorganization of the BEF's divisions into nine instead of twelve battalions. Ludendorff's strategy here was to smash down from the north-east and break the left flank of the Salient; in so doing he would cut behind the four divisions at Flesquières, the 51st, 17th, 63rd, and the 47th, putting 50,000 men 'in the bag' and removing the head of the salient, thus permitting his drive westwards unhindered. Eight German divisions had been concentrated in front of Flesquières.

Here was the Forward Zone and in front of it No Man's Land was about 400 yards deep, roughly, from where you are. The 63rd (Royal Naval) Division was here at the tip of the salient, with the 17th Division immediately on the left. The tour will attempt to follow the latter's front line. Beyond that was the 51st Division, whose position will also be seen. The 47th Division was over on the right, at Ribécourt. Two miles to the rear ran the Intermediate System, which was about a mile deep, from the front of Havrincourt to the dry Canal Du Nord; then began the three miles wide Battle Zone. Unfortunately this defence in depth, whilst a brilliant plan, was incomplete. Gough and Haig had been denied by the politicians (for reasons too complex to go into here) sufficient men to dig and complete it. There was only one reserve division available, the 2nd, based at the back of the Intermediate System in and about Havrincourt Wood. In the few days before the attack began on the 21st, Flesquières and the whole of the salient's point was drowned in poison gas, both phosgene and (for the first time) mustard; so bad was this that the 2nd Division

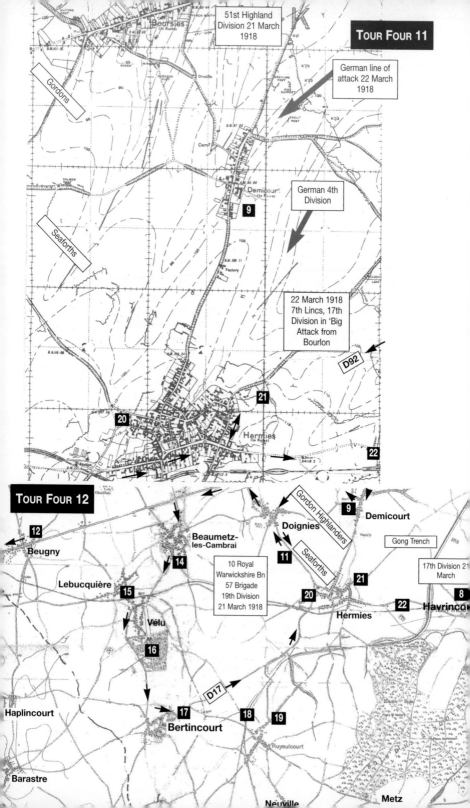

TOUR FOUR 11

51st Highland Division 21 March 1918

German line of attack 22 March 1918

Gordons

Seaforths

German 4th Division

Demicourt

9

22 March 1918 7th Lincs, 17th Division in 'Big Attack from Bourlon

D92

21

20

Hermies

22

TOUR FOUR 12

12

Beugny

Gordon Highlanders

Doignies

9

Demicourt

Beaumetz-les-Cambrai

11

Seaforths

Gong Trench

14

17th Division 21 March

Lebucquière

15

10 Royal Warwickshire Bn 57 Brigade 19th Division 21 March 1918

21

8

Vélu

20

Hermies

22

Havrinco

16

D17

Haplincourt

17

18

19

Bertincourt

Ruyaulcourt

Metz

Barastre

Neuville

had to be taken out of the line; the 17th and 47th were also badly hit. The 63rd, stationed here, where you are sitting, suffered 3,000 casualties, yet all three divisions had to stay. The Germans obviously hoped to drive the British out of Flesquières without having to attack, but the ploy failed. The three divisions at the tip of the salient, despite tremendous casualties, hung on until the evening of the 22nd. Then came a withdrawal from the village to a line behind the village of Havrincourt to the edge of the Canal du Nord and Havrincourt Wood.

Drive forward to the line held by the 17th Division, taking the road round the northern face of the village **(F)**. 52 Brigade (10/Lancashire Fusiliers, 9/Duke of Wellingtons, 12/Manchesters) was at the edge of the village, men of these battalions manning the track, then a trench facing north. There were a number of derelict British tanks here from November 1917. You can carry on this road which will take you under the autoroute, but the track at the far side may be unfit if the weather has been bad. Turn around and return to Flesquières and take the D92 to Havrincourt. In Havrincourt turn right on the D15; **(F)** on the map denotes the British front line on 21 March 1918. 51 Brigade, were further along the road, some distance beyond where the autoroute crosses the D15.

Stop at **(8)** on the bank which looks down to Lowrie Cemetery and over the Canal Du Nord, about 1,000 yards west. By 22 March 1918 the Germans had managed to force back the 17th Division towards Hermies, but the line had not been broken; to your right and in front were hundreds of German dead from the 234th Regiment's attack from Graincourt. Look towards the canal: to the right can be see the old factory buildings and Lock 7; and to the left a small wood on the far bank of the canal. That is an arrow head shaped fortress of the Hindenburg Line, the large hump of the Spoil Heap which 109 Brigade of the 36th (Ulster) Division had attacked on the 20 November 1917. Here, on both sides of the canal and filling the ground you can see was the Hindenburg Line, its many lines of trenches and barbed wire running north to south. After the British captured it in November 1917 they spent the next few months converting the German trenches for British use, altering fire steps and dugouts and the barbed wire barricades. The trenches received new names: nearby were, for example, London Trench, Jermyn Street, George Street and Knightsbridge; on the far side of the canal beyond the Spoil Heap were Key Trench, Gong Trench, Fagan Support and Lisclocher Lane.

50 Brigade was forward of here, the left of the division, the brigade's right flank, where the British front line crossed the dry canal. The Germans were aiming for Hermies, a village just over a couple of miles away from their grasp after they had broken through the Outpost Line. On 22 March they launched fierce attacks against Gong Trench **see Map T4 (12)**. The 7/East Yorks came under a heavy bombardment preparatory to the assault. Sergeant Harold Jackson volunteered for a daylight patrol, successfully getting in contact with the enemy and bringing back valuable information. Later the Germans succeeded in entering parts of the front line, but Sergeant Jackson forced them to withdraw. Later he stalked the enemy, destroying an enfilading machine gun post and killing its crew. A few days later, when all his officers had become casualties, he took command of his company, repeatedly going out under murderous fire to bring back badly wounded men. For his courage he was awarded the Victoria Cross.

Sergeant Harold Jackson VC

The tour will go to the area where his battle took place, but looking at this rather lovely scene, perhaps one of those elegant barges might be sailing past, it is difficult to imagine what is was like here then. Continue to drive along the D15, recalling that you are actually travelling through and along the Hindenburg Line. At the cross roads with the road from Graincourt, on the left is the canal bridge, then a ruin holding German machine gun nests, where the two Coldstream Guardsmen won their Victoria Crosses in September 1918.

On reaching the main road, the N30, turn left. The Germans were swarming around this area on 22 March 1918; at least 4,000 of them were heading for Hermies. It still had not fallen by the 23rd and the 17th Division's line still held, but it had withdrawn west of Flesquières and the dry canal.

The 51st (Highland) Division's position was centred about Boursies and its battle to maintain that part of the long flank of the Salient was becoming desperate. All of its three brigades were in the line (**see Battle Map 29**), 154 Brigade on the left of the road, 152 at Boursies with 153 on the right of the village. Very soon there is a junction with the D34b, turn left for Demicourt, then a total ruin. On either side of this country road were Germans attacking in the old style, in great waves, coming down over the main road, going south towards Hermies and towards the 17th Division's positions where, amongst others, Sergeant Jackson was battling. The Gordon Highlanders had an extremely effective

Vickers machine gun in action in this area which even without its tripod, was taking a heavy toll of the advancing foe. At the centre of the long narrow village turn right for Boursies and stop at **(9)**,the communal cemetery.

There are only ten men here, all killed in the last great drive to win the war in September 1918. Second Lieutenant Henry Reginald Burton was a veteran, commissioned from the Kings Company of the Grenadier Guards and killed with the Duke of Cornwall's Light Infantry on 11 September 1918. The graves of Corporal W Harrison and Gunner P MacDonald are evidence of the consequence of a direct hit on an 18-pdr Field Gun of 75 Brigade RFA on 27 September 1918.

Continue towards Boursies, but take the right fork before the village towards the N30 and there turn left. This is the middle of the 51st Division's fighting withdrawal on the 21st of March 1918. Drive slowly through the village and half way through stop at the French War Memorial **(10)**. It is salutary to be reminded of the suffering and of the contribution of the French army and people.

On leaving the village look to the right; it was here that 1/7th and 1/8th Black Watch of 153 Brigade were swallowed up by the enormous number of the enemy.

French War Memorial at Boursies.

Proceed to **(12)**, the Louverval Memorial to the Missing, with a small cemetery attached, but take the small road immediately before the Memorial (be very careful of the traffic hurtling behind you) into the small village and go to the end of it. Read the appropriate section in the battle narrative about the fighting here, often neglected. This was the battlefield of the Black Watch, the Germans advancing from the right. The Australians first captured the village at dawn on 2 April 1917. It was retaken in September 1918.

Return towards the main road, but park ON THE SIDE ROAD near the Memorial and walk to it.

In 1927 only 82 graves were made here, men brought in from the village chateau and seven German graves were removed. There are now 118 men buried here (six unknown – all Highlanders). These unknown, with 138 Germans were originally buried in the German cemetery which then existed at the eastern end of the village's chateau.

The memorial commemorates the 7,004 men whose bodies were never identified from the Battle of Cambrai. In the beautifully laid out cemetery below the Memorial are men from various regiments and corps. There is a Naval surgeon in A 35, Frank Pearce Pocock DSO,MC, aged twenty-seven, who was the Medical Officer on *Iris II* during the raid on Zeebrugge. Besides Australians, found in cemeteries across the Western Front, there is a New Zealander. The New Zealand Division was a fine formation, one of the most effective in the BEF, but about which too little is popularly known. A chaplain lies in plot A Grave 6, the Reverend Thomas Jasper Shovel from Linkinhorne, Cornwall. There's a moving epitaph, simple in its poignancy, on a London man's grave: 'Netty's Chum'.

Return (with great care!) towards Boursies. Just before the village turn sharp right, the road to Doignies. Go slowly here. It was the scene of savage fighting by the Gordons and the 1/5th Seaforths. In the village go left along the D34 (towards Hermies) for about half a mile; at the second track **(11)** turn round and stop. Here were Lieutenant J.G. Marks and Captain Clarke of the 6th Gordons. Coming towards them were Germans armed with flamethrowers, a fearsome weapon. The British had placed a Vickers machine gun here to fire along the main street of Doignies. The enemy in their hundreds were coming towards you from the right, Boursies. Gradually the Highlanders withdrew towards Beaumetz, west of here and then to Lebucquière.

Before driving back, north, to Doignies look to the left. There was 57 Brigade of the 19th Division, which had been hurriedly brought up to help the 17th and 51st. The 8/Gloucesters were practically annihilated coming forward, and the Worcesters and Warwicks suffered almost equally as badly as the enemy swept westwards, these battalions fighting with the Scots. For example, Major Johnstone handed over 300 Worcesters to 1/5th Seaforths' CO, Lieutenant Colonel JM Scott. The battlefield here is little known; and there is little to see unless you walk in the fields in the autumn and winter noting seemingly insignificant dips and hollows in the ground when the crops are off.

Drive back through the village and take the road to the left, the D34, to the N30. Turn left and stop at **(13)**, Beaumetz Cemetery No 1. It is stark evidence of the fighting here in the spring of 1918. There are 257 graves here but 182 are unidentified. It was made by the enemy after the fighting in March 1918; 307 of their dead were removed after the war. The majority of the British graves are Highlanders; Wherever you look are Gordons, Black Watch and Seaforths and numbers of Gloucesters. It is only a small cemetery but indicates the desperation of the struggle to contain the Germans on both sides of the road, the land so open and devoid of cover and the enemy artillery having a grandstand view of the British divisions in that week of March. A German account of these few days noted:

> *Thoughts of Verdun came back to recollection. Can it be that the attack has run itself to a standstill on the second day, watches show that it is 2pm, not a move relieves the horrible stagnation.*

Take the road on the left to Beaumetz and keep to the east of the village and stop at **(14)** Crossroads Cemetery, where 275 lie, (99 unidentified). The village was on fire and under intense German bombardment when the Seaforths and 152 Brigade withdrew here on 23

March 1918. After the Armistice 213 men were brought here from their battlefield graves and an American soldier was removed to their cemetery at Bony. There are Australians here from their victorious attacks into the Hindenburg Line of April 1917 and those who advanced to victory in 1918. There are many gunners from March 1918, casualties from shelling by the superior German artillery and from attempts to withdraw without losing guns.

In row F, close to the seat against the rear wall, in Grave 24 is Brigadier General Gilbert Follet DSO, MVO, Croix de Guerre, aged 40, commanding 3 Guards Brigade, killed on 27 September 1918. Obviously he is yet another example of a general not tucked away in a chateau well behind the lines. There are men from the Worcesters' March fighting, and the Guards (September 1918). There is a middle-aged Australian of 43 in row E Grave 7: Private Charles Stringfellow from Grenfell, New South Wales, serving with the 3rd Battalion Australian Infantry when he was killed in April 1917. Near him is a 40 year old gunner. In row F Grave 19 is Private Sidney Humphrey, a native of Weymouth, who relinquished a good position in Penang, the Straits Settlements (now Malaysia) who volunteered and enlisted in Wellington, New Zealand, serving with the 2nd Canterbury Regiment.

Take the left fork northwards towards Beaumetz and then turn left onto the D18E to Lebucquière and **(15)**, the large British plot behind part of the old communal cemetery, lying just south of the village, on the road to Vélu. The village, a smoking ruin in March 1918, was defended heroically by the 19th (Western) Division until it was overwhelmed on 23 March 1918. Whatever was the eventual outcome of the German attack, they failed to succeed in their pincer movement at Flesquières because of these divisions on the northern flank. There are 754 burials here (266 unknown). At the Armistice the cemetery contained only 150 graves.

At the top is the Great Cross Of Sacrifice and on either side of it are Special Memorials. As you walk down the central path you will come to plot II on the right and there, in row B Grave 21, lies a man who, captured in 1916, died here as a PoW on 9 July 1916. Lieutenant Colonel FHS Rendall DSO, who had commanded 5/York and Lancs, was 37 and was previously of the Duke of Corwall's Light Infantry. He came from Bodmin. Near him in row F grave 24 is a very young soldier who enlisted into the Royal Fusiliers in September 1914 and was then commissioned into the Royal West Kents and later attached to 20/Manchesters. Second Lieutenant RK Matheson (son of Sir Alexander and Lady Matheson) was exactly 18 when he was captured at Ginchy (on the Somme) on 3 September 1916 but died here from wounds just five days later. There are many men from the 42nd (East Lancs) Division in their advance to victory in September 1918 amongst them is Captain HL Murgatroyd MC, aged 23, 1/7th Lancashire Fusiliers, dying here on the 27th of that month from wounds suffered in the advance across the front face of Beaucamps. Major PC Edwards DCM of the 15th Royal Warwicks had joined up from his home in New Zealand; he was an old soldier who had seen many battles, serving in the South African campaign and then Gallipoli. He was commissioned from the ranks, and was killed here on 27 September 1918, aged 39, leaving his wife at 'Chanak Bahr' (a name resonant to New Zealanders who fought on Gallipoli), Leamington Spa.

Take the road round the western side of Vélu Wood **(16)**, always an awful place of dead and wounded men and horses, where hand to hand fighting took place in that week of March 1918. Continue slowly down to Bertincourt. The flat land surrounding Bertincourt contained a number of airfields. Turn left at the first left turning at the northern edge of the village. Chateau Cemetery **(17)** was visited on Tour 1. However, look to your right (south) and consider the scene on 22 – 24 March 1918. The valorous 17th Division had hung on to their Havrincourt-Hermies line, assisted by the 19th; the 51st was almost 'spent' as was the 2nd, but they had defied the enemy's attack, thus allowing the battered 63rd and the 47th Divisions to withdraw from the salient through here and below at Ytres. Think of the Casualty Clearing Stations two miles below Ytres (locations seen on Tour 1), many hundreds of wounded in their bloodied and filthy uniforms, lying out on stretchers whilst hundreds more were arriving from the battles in progress with the Germans just behind them, shelling their approach. What panic there must have been here, roads congested, nursing staff trying to get the casualties to the west, not knowing where 'safety' was, unable to attend to most of their patients. Some valiant doctors and nurses would be carrying out operations on terribly wounded men that could not wait.

Follow the road to the left and take the D7 to Ruyaulcourt. Just before the village there is a track going off to the left, signed to the northern end of the Canal Du Nord tunnel **(18)**. Proceed there, a most interesting place. The tunnel was filled with water but held in by a dam.

The British cemetery in the sunken road **(19)** has previously been visited. Take the D19E to the north which crosses the canal and then turn right for Hermies. This road was jammed with German dead who had been killed coming towards you on 23 March 1918, slaughtered by lorry mounted machine guns. Two cemeteries **(20)** are sited on opposite sides of the road on the south west corner of the village.

In the small cemetery on the left, Hermies British Cemetery, there are only 108 graves (three unidentified). Three rows up from the gate, in row F, is Brigadier General Roland Boys Bradford VC, MC, aged 25, originally of the DLI. He won his Victoria Cross in November 1916 in the area of the Butte de Warlencourt. In the same row, Grave 3, you will find the Reverend George Ranking; he was 46, attached to IV Corps Heavy Artillery. He left a wife at Haslemere. In row C there is a pilot, Second Lieutenant AS Morgan of the RFC, aged 29 and from Birmingham. He had previously served with the South African Division's Signal company in German South West Africa.

Cross the road into Hermies Hill Cemetery, with 1,005 graves (297 unknown). Four small cemeteries were removed from their wartime location near here and gathered in to this one. You will see from the register that the original burials were in plot I, which occupies the top right hand quarter, just below the Great Cross of Sacrifice; the Special Memorials are also there. The remaining three plots, holding 819 graves, were made after the Armistice. Consider the enormously fraught task of the Graves Registration Battalions that scoured the battlefields after the war.

Second Lieutenant Frank Edward Young VC lies in plot III

Brigadier General Roland Boys Bradford VC

Second Lieutenant Frank Edward Young VC

row B grave 5, a few yards up the central path, in the eighth row on the right. He was 23 and serving with 1/Hertfords when he was killed on 18 September 1918; his long citation (as is that for all VC winners buried in a particular cemetery) is in the Register. Another formidable soldier was Sergeant Frank Mossop DCM and Bar, MM. Aged only 21 he came from Pennsylvania USA but served with 1/King's Liverpools. He was killed on 26 December 1917 and now lies in plot I row F Grave 37, fairly close to the right hand wall.

Before you leave, when you are close to the gate, stop at row G on the right, the third row from the entrance. In Grave 6 is a 26 years old man, Private Leonard Long of the Northumberland Fusiliers. He was wounded on the Somme and died here as a PoW on 20 November 1916. The awful tragedy for his parents in Stockport is that he was one of three brothers who were all killed.

Turn right into the village. At the green the Australians found a huge German mine crater when they captured the battered village. Go slowly as you head for Havrincourt on the D5; at the last crossroads on the eastern side of the village turn left up a narrow track, a country lane, it curves like a shallow letter 'S' **(21)** and then the track goes north-east into open rolling country. It is usually not fit for a car after a few yards but stop and consider 50 Brigade's battle here. If you walk 200 yards up the track you are at Lurgan Avenue, a trench running across your front where the 6/Dorsets and 10/West Yorks fought on 22 March 1918. Proceed a further 600 yards, it will only take you about ten minutes to walk, to the site of Gong Trench. It was here that 7/East Yorks battled and Sergeant Harold Jackson earned his Victoria Cross. It would be a pity not to make the effort to get here as so often the sites of such heroic efforts have been completely altered and hidden by progress. Consider the turmoil and desperation here that morning, in daylight, when both brave German and British soldiers, probably a couple of thousand or so within a quarter of a mile all around you, fought to survive.

Take the road for Havrincourt **(22)**. Before crossing the bridge over the gorge, stop at the small scrap yard on the left. A track leads along the high bank of the canal to the Spoil Heap, looking very much like it must have done in 1917 but now covered in shrubbery. Maxwell Avenue trench ran along the right hand side of the road towards the bridge; whilst a few yards on the western side of it was a ring of trenches, South, West and North.

It is a simple matter to return to base via Havrincourt and the N30.

Location of Gong Trench. Looking west from Canal du Nord. Hermies on left skyline.

TOUR FIVE

This tour covers the final battle for Flesquières in the last week of September 1918 and a visit to two cemeteries in Cambrai.

Battle Maps: 34, 35, 36, 37   Tour circuit distance: **20 miles**.

This is the final tour; it is essentially a cemeteries tour, as the ground has been covered in earlier visits. Proceed to Anneux Military Cemetery **(1)**, south of Bourlon Wood on the N30.

The Cross of Sacrifice and the War Stone are at opposite ends of the cemetery. At the back is a long row of 87 Special Memorials. A large number of the unknown must have fallen in or near Bourlon Wood and there are 72 'known' men from this fighting. In Special Memorial No. 3 you will find commemorated Lieutenant John Allison of the Argylls, commissioned from the ranks in 1915. Lieutenant Noel Douglas Bayly (III F 7) of the Irish Guards was killed at Fontaine when aged 28; his father had been a major in the Gordons. There is a cavalryman in plot IV row A Grave 6, Private WC Butcher of the Royal Scots Grays, killed when in the dismounted role on 27 November 1917; another lies in plot III row F Grave 79, Sergeant George Carr of the 1st King Edward's Horse, who had served in South Africa. Lance Corporal Harold Chadwick, aged eighteen, had gone into the wood with 19/Royal Welch Fusiliers and now lies in plot III row B Grave 8 and seems to be the youngest soldier here. In plot IV row A Grave 8 is an Australian who could have died as a prisoner of war. Private AW Croft of the 4th Infantry Battalion died on 15 April 1917 aged 34. He was probably captured either at Hermies or Moeuvres. Perhaps his body was not found until after the war, or was brought in from a small battlefield cemetery. In plot I row E Grave 31 is Captain CM Dunn, aged 23, twice Mentioned in Despatches and killed in November 1917. Quite close to the gate, in plot I row F Grave 12 is the 35 years old Second Lieutenant FG Wheatcroft, 13/East Surrey's, a schoolmaster and one time professional footballer.

Turn left towards Anneux village. Take the road through it to the right, heading for Graincourt. Proceed through here on D15E (the Demicourt road), cross the D15 and cross the canal bridge. Park here (you have not got much choice!) The bridge you have crossed is where the Germans built a machine gun nest on the east side, under the rubble of the destroyed bridge, causing havoc amongst the assaulting 2 Guards Brigade, particularly 1/Coldstream. Captain CH Frisby and four men, including Lance Corporal TN Jackson, got through the barbed wire strewn canal bottom and wiped out the German position. The two were awarded the Victoria Cross, as mentioned before. It is one of the rare places where two VCs were awarded for the same action. The large mound is worth an exploration – there are remnants of bunkers there. Half a mile down the canal side road is Sanders Keep Cemetery where Jackson now lies. The view from the western side of the canal of the gently rising slope on the opposite side gives a tremendous impression of what the depth of barbed wire in front of a Hindenburg Line trench must have looked like. Standing at the cemetery, if you have time, you can see the open land and the slope from the canal that the Guards had to advance over, giving a German perspective.

Return to the crossroads with the D15 and head for Havrincourt; you are in 3rd Division country. Looking to your right, you can see where Bradford was killed. When you

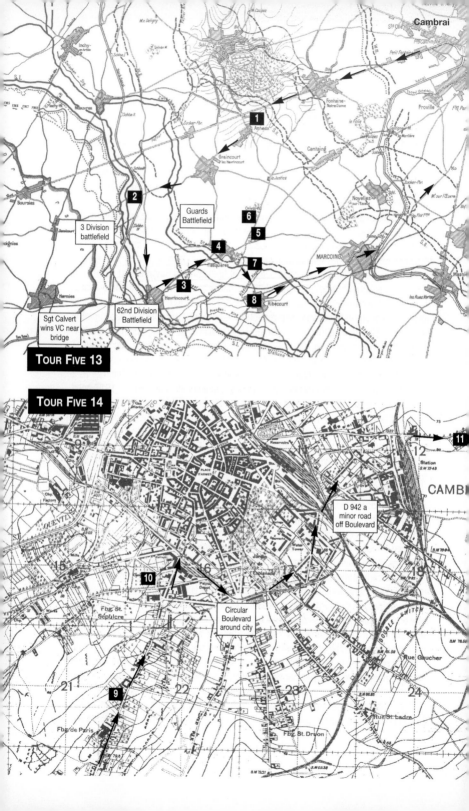

TOUR FIVE 13

3 Division battlefield

Guards Battlefield

62nd Division Battlefield

Sgt Calvert wins VC near bridge

TOUR FIVE 14

D 942 a minor road off Boulevard

Circular Boulevard around city

cross the autoroute and are almost in Havrincourt pause for a moment. A third Victoria Cross was awarded near here to Sergeant Leonard Calvert for his action in eliminating a German strong point in the 2/5th KOYLIs advance of 12 September 1918 on Havrincourt. The site may be seen by going down the road to Trescault but then turning right for Hermies and Vesuvius, the strong point seen on an earlier tour west of the bridge. This is in the 62nd (West Riding) Division's battlefield on 12 September 1918 when, well in advance of VI Corps, they captured Havrincourt.

In Havrincourt head out on the D92 for Flesquières. Go slowly and stop at **(3)**. Here are the remains of the railway embankment where the strong enemy position stopped any further advance of the Yorkshiremen on the 12th. You have a magnificent view from here of all the battles of the Flanders Sanatorium in November and December 1917, March 1918 and again in September of the same year. You can see across the bowl as far as Beaucamps, with Trescault half way across on the right; a fertile imagination might envisage the tank attack. In 1918 it was the 3rd Division who would take Flesquières.

On the left was 8 Brigade. Passing you on the right were the Fusiliers and the King's Liverpools of 9 Brigade, who would take the southern edge of the village; and down in the bottom of the valley was 127 Brigade (Manchesters) advancing on the 42nd Division's left flank. Way over on the far slope the Lancashire Fusiliers of 125 Brigade's advance were being mown down by the enemy's machine guns in Beaucamps whilst the 5th Division of IV Corps struggled to take the village.

At the start of Flesquières take the left fork. This is in the area of 76 Brigade's attack with tanks. The Gordons and the Suffolks fought to clear the bitterly defended ruin of a village. At the church **(4)** stop in front of the Mairie with its French War Memorial. Captain Lee and sixty Gordons fought through here, going to your left and the northern edge of the village to get in touch with the Irish Guards. Lee would be awarded the DSO. Turn left at the T junction and stop at the village green. At the brick wall on the corner was the old watering point where cavalry and men used the water filled depression; shrapnel and bullet marks can be seen in the bricks.

Drive forward and stop by the Flesquières Hill Military Cemetery. At the fork of the road just beyond is the site of the Sugar Beet Factory **(5)**. Consider this last battle here on 26th/27 September 1918. Looking at the size and position of the factory (now a farm) it is no wonder the defenders held off the attacking Guards Division and the Yorkshire Division's 185 Brigade, coming through to take over from the 3rd Division, for some time. The village streets were strewn with some hundreds of British casualties then. Later the Guards and Yorkshiremen had advanced for more than a mile beyond Orival Wood and were astride the road running to the right, the D92. They were driven back by the fierceness of the German counter-attack from Premy Chapel Hill.

Return to the crossroads (nearby *Deborah* was knocked out), turn left and pass the barn on the left where the two flags are flying and where, today, the recovered *Deborah* sits, the only tank from the battle actually to drive on the cobbles of Cambrai. The city donated these for the platform on which the tank now rests.

Go straight across towards Ribécourt down the hill, passing the scene of the tank disaster on 20 November 1917 as they attacked up the hill **(7)**. At Ribécourt **(8)** turn left along the D29 for Marcoing, the battlefield of the 29th Division during the last week of November 1917 and where they faced the German counter-attack of the 30th. Drive into the large village, turn right at a T junction, following the signs for the D56 and Cambrai.

Crossroads in Flesquières where the tank D51 *Deborah* was knocked out. The recovered tank is on display in a barn in the village. Looking southwards and the direction from which the Highlanders'attacked the village.

Go left at the roundabout and a few hundred yards will bring you to a bridge over the St Quentin Canal. Drive slowly and turn right, you will see the railway station high up on the bank on the left, drive round the curve and stop at the disused railway bridge. One can see the old bridge alongside the new one. It was here that Sergeant Spackman of 1/Border Regiment charged across the 'old' bridge on 20 November 1917 to eliminate with rifle and bayonet the German machine gun post on the railway platform. He was awarded the Victoria Cross. At the time of writing very little has changed.

Left: the old railway bridge which Spackman charged (towards the camera) was still there in 2003. Below: Marcoing railway station where the German machine gun was set up on the platform.

Turn round now, drive back down the hill and continue on the D56 for Cambrai. After two miles the road will join the N44 and at **(9)** you will pass the Hotel Beatus; go slowly now, very close to the hospital on the left is a turning, a short street, it leads to the very large Porte de Paris Communal Cemetery where there is a British section **(10)**. You can park alongside the wall on the quiet street and there is an entrance half way down. It is an enormous cemetery but head for the French Tricolour on its tall white pole. Nearby are the British military graves. All of them were buried most respectfully by the Germans during their long occupation of Cambrai. At one time the cemetery contained 1,521 German graves, but they were removed after the war. The register records 113 British dead of which 93 are British soldiers (with only nine unknown); there are ten Canadians, seven Australians, one New Zealander, one South African and six Belgian civilians. The grave stones are weathered and difficult to read. The majority died as prisoners of war and at least six of them are from 1914. There is one RNAS officer from the UK. Alongside the path, close to the eastern wall and about half way along its length, is the extremely unusual New Zealander's private grave, large and impressive, of a reddish brown stone. Here lies Second Lieutenant DG McMillann MC, aged twenty-five, killed on 28 September 1918. He came from New Zealand with the New Zealand Artillery and had served in Samoa and on Gallipoli. He was so close to returning to Wellington after four years of war. Major HC Johnston DSO of the Kings Royal Rifle Corps, captured at Le Cateau in August 1914 died as a prisoner of war on 1 January 1915. He lies in plot I row A Grave 14. In plot 1 row A Grave 4 is Private AF Patterson of the 16/HLI, wounded at Beaumont Hamel (possibly in the heroic defence of Frankfurt Trench) and dying here on 29 November 1916, fifty miles from his fatal battle. There are a number of fliers here; and in plot II row B Grave 22 is another Patterson, a Second Lieutenant in the RFC, shot down on 25 September 1916 and dying of his wounds. Sergeant P Snowden of 45 Squadron RFC was aged 22 when he was shot down on 22 October 1916. He came from Ravensthorpe, Yorkshire. Take the time to visit the French military section of the cemetery.

Return to the major road and turn left towards the town. At the major junction with the Circular Boulevard turn right but drive slowly and keep on the right; you are looking for a rather small but main road going off to the right to Solesmes. Take care, I have missed the turning and I know the town well. You will eventually come to a T junction with the N43 going south-east, turn left and at the next cross roads go right onto the D942. There is a small sign post to Solesmes but it is easily overshot and it is not a major road. You will cross over the railway at a bridge, go very slowly and immediately on the right is a stone wall and a small parking place **(11)**, stop. This is Cambrai East Military Cemetery. This vast cemetery is awe inspiring and overwhelmingly German. It is very stark and filled with graves holding more than one man. There are 10,000 German burials, of which 2,746 are unknown. After the war the French wanted the German dead concentrated to a few cemeteries and this was one of those and thousands were brought here. The Bavarian Commandant of the town buried here men of whatever nationality in the most respectful way. Each had their own plots, identified by a helmet of their type cast into a stone marker. Realising in September 1918 he would soon lose the town, he recorded that he had handed over the cemetery to the French authorities for its safe keeping and maintenance. Some of it was damaged in subsequent fighting and during the Second World War. There are more than 500 British graves in two plots, one close to the gate which contains graves of British prisoners of war and the other made up of six plots in the top right hand, eastern corner, holding sixty-nine graves from battlefields east of the town. Over on the right is a large plot holding some hundreds of French graves, most of them with Russian names. A few might have belonged to the Russian Legion who, true to the pact with the French made before the war began, came through England on their way to fight alongside their French allies. Most were German prisoners who were used as labourers. The square plot close to the gate (VII) contains seventy-one men, mostly dying as prisoners. One of the first men I found was from my home town, Burnley. Private Walter Scott, aged thirty-eight, of the 2/East Lancs died on 25 August 1918, the husband of Elizabeth of 10 Goulridge Street. He lies in plot VII row B Grave 19, just along the left hand border. Close to him lies Private HG Joy of 3/Grenadiers, mortally wounded at Fontaine on 27 November 1917 and now in Grave 7. In the top corner is a Special Memorial to Private James Revell of the 1/East Lancs, buried here on 24 October 1916, probably captured on the Somme.

When you have visited the men here near the gate, walk across the cemetery and notice the shell fragment marks on some of the monuments. Over on the right are the concrete crosses of the French/Russian graves and in the top right hand corner are more British burials. In plot I row A Grave 4, almost on the eastern border, is Lieutenant Leslie Young, aged 19, of 25 Squadron RAF, dying here on the 24 October 1918. In plot III, against the eastern border, is the only American, aged 20 from Delaware, who served with the Connaught Rangers. He died of influenza in December 1918.

War is tragic; and a grave here underlines that. In plot I row A Grave 38 lies Corporal FG Potter, aged nineteen, of 1/5th West Yorks who died of wounds on 1 November 1918. His brother, fighting elsewhere on the Western Front, fell on the same day. The people at home at 41, Mildmay Park, London would have heard the news just about the time that the Armistice was declared.

Memorial stones to the French, British and German dead intered in Cambrai East Military Cemetery. These show scaring damage from the Second World War.

INDEX